Sewing
with Oilcloth

Kelly McCants

WILEY

Wiley Publishing, Inc.

NOV 2011

Credits

Senior Editor
Roxane Cerda

Project Editor
Charlotte Kughen,
The Wordsmithery LLC

Editorial Manager
Christina Stambaugh

**Vice President
and Publisher**
Cindy Kitchel

**Vice President and
Executive Publisher**
Kathy Nebenhaus

Interior Design
Erin Zeltner

Cover Design
Wendy Mount

Photography
Meghan McSweeney

Graphics
Cheryl Grubbs
Brent Savage
Laura Campbell
Rashell Smith

Acknowledgments

I must say that this dreamy endeavor was a true labor of love, and I couldn't have done it without my family, friends, and my great team of experts!

Roxane Cerda, you are spectacular. Thank you for believing in me and getting my oilcloth addiction out to the world. Charlotte Kughen, your patience and mad editing skills are exactly what a first-time writer needs. Thank you both for holding my hand every step of the way. Stefanie Von Borstel, at Full Circle Literary, thanks for guiding me through my first book with ease and grace. It was an honor and a pleasure to work with you all. To Meghan McSweeney, my photographer, I can't thank you enough! You're talented beyond measure and a joy to work with. Your spirit is just as lovely as your photos.

To my husband, Don, thank you for knowing more about trim and notions than any nonsewer on the planet. Thank you for all those last-minute trips to the fabric shop. Thank you for surprising me with special caffeinated and chocolaty treats—those treats and your hugs got me through the many late nights that led up to my deadlines. Most importantly, I need to thank you for being honest about the projects in this book. Your opinions and suggestions are the reasons why the projects got better with every mock-up! You're the best Mr. Modern June a girl could hope for! I love you.

To my great kids, Maddie and Aidan, thank you for cheering me through the long work days and sleepy mornings. Thanks for giving each project your seal of approval with such enthusiasm. The support and patience you give me every day makes me proud to be your momma. You inspire me to follow my dreams—I do what I do both "because of" and "for" you.

To my Junies, I know each one of you lovely ladies has had my back every step of the way! Thank you, Dawn Anderson, Kathy Longbricco, Nicole Lee, Ono Mangano-Parent, Amy Martinez, Jennifer Dyson, Mary Carley, and last, but not least, Janet Devoss. Honestly, I couldn't do it without you all! To my mommy-friends who helped me problem-solve, listened to me kvetch, and hugged me when I needed it most. What can I say? *Most* of what happens at the picnic table stays at the picnic table!

A big thanks goes out to my wonderful models—thanks for making this book shine. To Ono Mangano-Parent, who wore sweaters in the heat and bare arms in the cold, thank you! To Kirsten and Miriam Schueler, thank you for icing cookies for me and making me smile. To Baby Leo Kim, what can I say? You're just dreamy in every way possible. To my lunch buddies, Owen and Emerson Ayers, thank you for eating up a few snacks for me. To my dear, sweet daughter Maddie, who lent a hand and a shoulder when we needed you most!

A special thanks to the following people who helped me visualize the projects: Marc and Tony of Feathernesters, thank you for your support over the last five wonderful years. You were the first to believe in Modern June and that still means the world to me. Thanks for letting us crash your gorgeous shop to take some wonderful pictures. Thanks to my neighbor Susie for the use of her lovely front porch and to SewOno.com for lending us some lovely Eco Apparel. A big thanks goes out to Carolyn Boutchyard Young for the days that she offered up her gorgeous home and farm; your kindness and hospitality are inspiring.

Lastly, I would like to thank my Grr (Grandmother Lewis). You made my childhood a happy one. Thank you for the late-night games, the trips to the library, the no-bake chocolate oatmeal cookies, and my love of aprons. If it weren't for your aqua gingham apron, there wouldn't be a Modern June. I miss you every single day! This book is for you, Grr.

XOXOXO,

Kelly

Wiley Publishing would like to thank the following people for their invaluable help in testing projects in this book prior to publication:

- Melanie Tenore, who can be found at her website at www.projectanthologies.com
- April Kennedy
- April Forshee
- Nicole Lee

Table of Contents

Introduction

I first discovered oilcloth in 2006 after an acquaintance mentioned that she was making oilcloth seat cushions (see page 42 for the seat cushion project) for the kitchen nook of her 1950s colonial. I never laid eyes on her kitchen, but just the sound of it sparked a fire that has led up to this very book. For months, I searched high and low in local fabric shops as I looked for oilcloth to no avail. Finally after an Internet search and an online buy later, I was hooked.

At first I made market totes to sell at the Farmers Market, and then I made aprons. By the next year I was a full-fledged "Oilcloth Addict," thriving on the challenge of finding new projects for the slick stuff. Nothing makes me happier than finding something new to do with oilcloth! So here, just for you, I have created 20 fresh new projects to make with oilcloth and its close cousins laminated cotton and chalk cloth.

Oilcloth has evolved a lot over the centuries. In the Middle Ages through the Civil War, oilcloth was made with an expensive but sturdy cotton fabric that was coated in layers and layers of various oils. Oilcloth was used to cover windows, tables, roofs, and floors, as well as for making sturdy waterproof clothing. During the Industrial Revolution, factories began manufacturing a more modern and resilient oilcloth by permeating cotton mesh with vinyl. Victorian women could order ready-made oilcloth for 15 cents a yard from the Sears and Roebuck catalog. By the early 1900s the Standard Table Oilcloth Company became the largest manufacturer of oilcloth in the world, and rolls of oilcloth were displayed alongside other fabrics of the day. In the 1930s, publications such as *Popular Mechanics* published projects for oilcloth that included room dividers, doorstops, and shoe organizers. Later in the 1950s, women all over the U.S. headed off to their local five-and-dimes to get oilcloth for their tables, shelves, and other crafty endeavors.

Today, most oilcloth found in the U.S. is imported from Mexico. Its bright and bold prints have existed south of the border for decades, but they are as fresh and festive for our modern homes as they were 50 years ago. Today's oilcloth is a PVC product (meaning it contains polyvinyl chloride). It's waterproof and sturdy so it wears long and hard.

Oilcloth contains phthalates and is not to be used for projects intended for children under the age of 12—so for those projects I use laminated cotton. Laminated cotton is a rather new fabric to the market. It's a friendly fabric for children's projects and food items, and it is CPSIA (Consumer Product Safety Improvement Act) compliant. This thinner and more supple oilcloth is a high-quality quilt-weight cotton print that's coated with a thin layer of polyurethane on the fabric's right side. Along with both types of oilcloth projects, I've included some that require chalk cloth, which is another vinyl product you can use as a chalkboard surface.

In my five years of selling my Modern June oilcloth wares and Oilcloth Addict yardage, I have heard some of the most amazing stories. As my customers touch and feel oilcloth, it takes them back in time. They speak of their mothers, aunts, and grandmothers. They recall family trips to Woolworth's to get a new oilcloth for the kitchen table. One woman said that her mother went to Woolworth's every year for a new roll of oilcloth, while another's mom went only when her oilcloth was worn and torn. I was told by one man that he had "eaten many a bad meal on oilcloth." My kids can say the same thing, as I am a designer but not a cook. For me, oilcloth is all about making memories, and to me the greatest thing in the world is living a life full of happy memories. I hope this book and its projects will help you create an even happier home, filled with exciting celebrations and all the comfort of new and old traditions using oilcloth.

Many crafty thanks,

Kelly

I'd love to share your finished projects on the flickr page dedicated to Sewing with Oilcloth. *For details check out modernjune.blogspot.com or oilclothaddict.blogspot.com.*

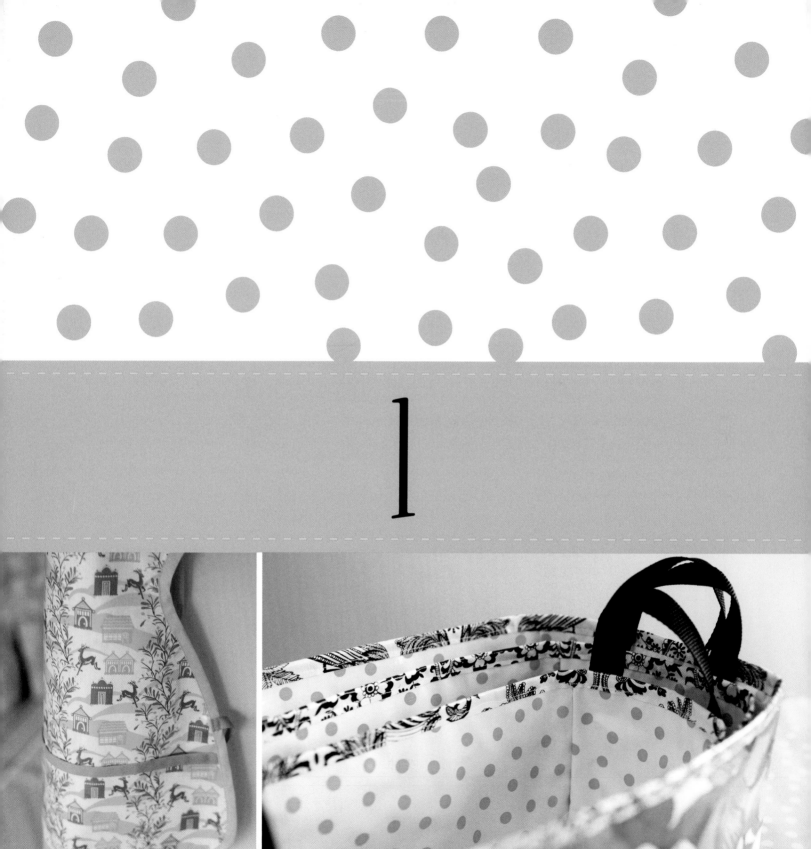

1

Tools, Tips, and Trims

orking with new fabrics can be a fun challenge for the seasoned stitcher, and it might be a bit intimidating for the novice sewer. Whichever category you fit into I am here to encourage and guide you through the useful projects in this book. Sewing with oilcloth is no different than sewing anything else as long as you have the right tools for the job and my handy tips at your side.

Tools

"Super H" Presser Foot: This is what I call the Open Embroidery foot; it's commonly included with the purchase of sewing machines, so you probably have it. I like to use this when I am attaching trim or edge stitching. It enables me to see exactly where I am sewing.

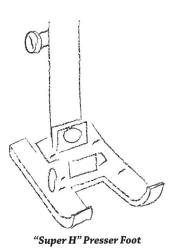

"Super H" Presser Foot

Roller or Nonstick Foot: Rollers or nonstick presser feet are very helpful, especially when topstitching on oilcloth. These specialty feet have rollers or a Teflon coating on their soles to glide over the sticky surface of oilcloth and laminated cotton.

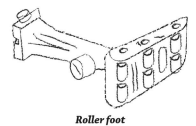

Roller foot

Presser Foot Tape Tip: If you are just getting started and you don't have a fancy roller or nonstick presser foot, don't fret. Try applying a bit of painter's or masking tape to the bottom of your regular feet. Cover the sole of the foot with tape, and then carefully use a craft knife to trim off any tape that isn't touching the metal.

Double-stick Tape: Using double-stick tape is a great trick when you're trying to avoid pins. I love to use it when appliquéing oilcloth.

Clear Ruler: This is one of the handiest tools for the modern sewer. A wide, clear ruler not only helps you measure; it helps you create square corners. Choose a clear ruler that has a marking for 45° angles to help you create oilcloth bias strips.

Rotary Cutter: A rotary cutter is an indispensable tool. When you couple it with a cutting mat and a clear ruler you're sure to get straight cuts.

Cutting Mat: This is essential when using rotary cutters. The cutting mat protects your work surface and keeps your blades sharp.

Pattern Weights: An alternative to pinning, commercial or handmade pattern weights can help keep your patterns situated while you trace them.

Fabric Scissors: I use regular fabric scissors when cutting oilcloth. I do find that they dull faster than when I cut woven fabrics, so I keep another pair just for cottons.

Marking Tools: It's best to use a pencil when marking on the wrong side of oilcloth and laminated cotton. Pen ink can show through oilcloth in time, so never use a pen in the center of a pattern piece. The exception to the rule is when you're tracing patterns on chalk cloth. Pencil is very hard to see on either side of the fabric's dark surface. If you accidentally get pen on the right side of oilcloth, a bit of hair spray and a rag should save the day. Water-soluble fabric markers are perfect when marking stitch lines onto the right side of oilcloth. Be sure to test your fabric marker on a scrap and wipe it clean as quickly as possible.

Pins: I use several different pins when working with oilcloth. I use traditional dressmaking pins for most of my projects, but occasionally I find a quilting pin to be helpful if I am going through something thick. It's easier to push in and pull out. It might surprise you that I also find that clothespins or binder clips are indispensable when working with oilcloth; they can be helpful when cutting or when topstitching a hem. These clever gadgets keep you from getting pin holes in your projects. See the "Tips" section for more information on pinning.

Tracing Paper and Wheel: Use the tracing paper and wheel with a smooth edge to transfer stitch lines and darts to your fabric. Lay the carbon side of the tracing paper on the wrong side of the fabric and then layer your pattern on top of the tracing paper. Roll the tracing wheel over the seam line on the pattern, and you have the necessary stitch lines on your fabric.

Seam Gauge: A seam gauge is a ruler that enables you to measure fabric, but it includes a special slider that you can use to mark a desired measurement.

Tips

Caring for oilcloth: You can wipe oilcloth clean using a warm, soapy sponge. Machine washing is not suggested.

Caring for laminated cotton: Although manufacturers of laminated cotton suggest that we wipe laminated cotton with a damp cloth, some projects can be machine washed. If your project is small and unlined, it should be completely washable. Make sure to line dry.

Caring for chalk cloth: For best results you need to prep your chalk cloth before use. To cure your new chalk cloth, lay a piece of chalk on its side on the chalk cloth surface, and rub all over, side to side, and then wipe clean. Now, do this one more time rubbing your chalk up and down. Wipe it clean one last time, and the chalk cloth is now ready for use.

Storage: Store your oilcloth, laminated cotton, and chalk cloth material rolled. When you're done making pretty projects, store them by hanging them or rolling them after they are clean and dry.

Straight Topstitches: It's good to be picky about your stitches. So how do you get a super straight topstitch? The trick is to use the edge of your presser foot as your guide instead of the seam gauge on the machine's stitch plate. I simply line up the project to the presser foot and move the needle to the side until I have it where I need it. I seem to have more control and get a straighter stitch line. Topstitching on oilcloth and laminated cotton can be a sticky situation, literally, so use a roller or nonstick foot and lengthen the stitches to a 3-4. Also, proceed slowly. Even if you're a seasoned pro at sewing with woven fabrics, I suggest that you use a scrap of oilcloth that's equally thick as your project to practice until you get the hang of it.

Stitch Length: Oilcloth can move slowly through a sewing machine due to its sticky nature. A longer stitch length, 3-4, works nicely when edge stitching, understitching, or topstitching.

Matching Prints: Matching up your prints starts with knowing the fabric's repeat, which is where the new pattern begins. For example, the lace oilcloth repeats every 17". If you are particular about your prints matching up (as I can be) I recommend that you buy an extra ¼ to ¾ yard depending on your fabric choice.

Edge Stitch: When you're adding trim or understitching, edge stitching is a handy and professional technique to use. Using your "Super H" presser foot, move your needle position to the left. Line up the left side of the trim with the left, inner side of the H shape of the foot, and use the inside of the presser foot as a guide.

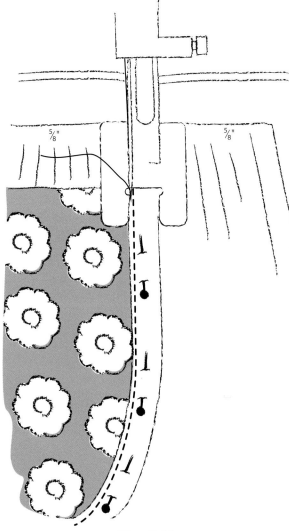

Edge stitching

Ironing Oilcloth: Ironing oilcloth is not recommended as it's a PVC and would melt if touched by the high heat of an iron. It's best to rely on less traditional means to press oilcloth and achieve professional-looking projects. The heat of the sun is great for taking out creases caused during shipping. Simply lay your oilcloth yardage out in the sun or hang it on the clothesline. The sun warms the plastic, thus softening it, and then you can roll the creased oilcloth tightly. After the oilcloth cools off, it will be less creased. If you've used a flat surface to warm up your oilcloth, you can use your hand to smooth out wrinkles as well. This is handy with smaller cuts of oilcloth. Any remaining creases dissipate with use.

Finger Press: Use your finger or the palm of your hand to smooth down a seam allowance or to crease a fold into your fabric. A few passes of your hand is all it takes to get the job done.

Crease Pressing Trim: When applying oilcloth trim to your project, it's helpful to crease press the trim first. Do so by folding your oilcloth trim in half and running the edges along the edge of a table. This makes a crease and acts as a guide when applying your trim to your oilcloth projects.

Book Press: Simply place a stack of books on the part of your project that needs a nice sharp crease and leave it overnight. Book pressing is great for pockets and any items that fold. This low-tech, simple way of pressing helps create a professional-looking project.

Ironing Laminated Cotton: You can iron laminated cotton if you take the right precautions. The number-one rule is to always use a press cloth, such as a clean white tea towel. Using two press cloths at a time is even better; use one to cover the ironing board and the second one to layer between the project and the iron. Ideally you want to press the laminated cotton from the wrong side of the fabric, but there are times when you need to press on the right side. In this instance, using a press cloth is a *must*. Never let your iron touch the thin layer of BPA- and PVC-free plastic or it will melt. Use a low temperature iron and skip the steam; a dry iron is best.

Avoiding Pin Holes: Straight pins can leave pin holes in oilcloth, so strategic pinning is a must. When laying out your patterns, avoid pinning through the oilcloth on the inside of the pattern piece the way you usually do with woven fabrics. I suggest pinning in the seam allowances or using pattern weights to secure your pattern while you trace it.

Creative Pinning: Binder clips, clothespins, and paper clips can be very handy to have around when you're working with oilcloth, chalk cloth, and laminated cotton, especially when it comes to topstitching. You can often use one of these items in place of pins that could leave holes in your fabric.

Understitching: Because oilcloth and laminated cottons shouldn't be ironed, I find that understitching is the key to flat seams. Simply finger press your seam toward the backside of your project and edge stitch it into place for a professional finish.

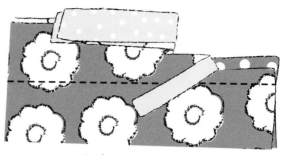

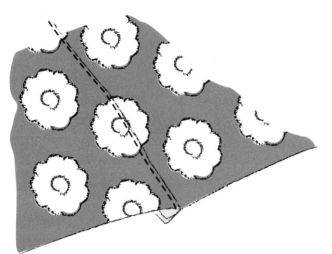

Understitching

Appliquéing with Oilcloth: Birds, cupcakes, and flowers . . . the possibilities for appliqués are endless. For simple appliqué patterns look for coloring book pages on the Internet. Monograms are easily created in a word processing program. Use an oilcloth with a floral print to create your own one-of-a-kind pillow by cutting out individual flowers and attaching them to your next project.

Glue: Glue sticks can be a helpful substitute for pins when working with laminated cotton. A thin layer of glue can keep two layers of laminated cotton together while you sew. Allow it to fully dry before sewing so your needle stays clean. Oilcloth, on the other hand, doesn't take to glue; as of the publication of this book I haven't found any glue that works with oilcloth. For example, I tried using hot glue to attach chalk cloth to oilcloth, but it fell off after a month.

Flat-line: Flat-lining is when you sew your lining and shell pieces of your project (with the wrong sides together) before you assemble. You then treat the flat-lined piece as one piece; flat-lining gives your fabric more heft so it functions better in a project. To flat-line, stitch the two layers together by basting all sides of the piece together. Be sure to baste within the seam allowance.

Grading seams allowances: You grade a seam allowance when you cut the seam allowances to different widths, as shown in the illustration. The seam allowance that falls nearest the garment side is cut the widest.

Grading a seam allowance

Trims

Cotton Bias: Many of the projects in this book require cotton bias tape. In all cases I suggest using prepackaged double-fold bias tape but only for the sake of practicality! Please feel free to make your own bias for unique, one-of-a-kind projects.

Connecting the cotton bias: It's easy to piece bias together after you've seen how to do it. Start by opening up the double-fold bias tape and placing the right sides together so that they create a 90° angle. Pin and sew a diagonal line. Cut off the extra, refold, and press.

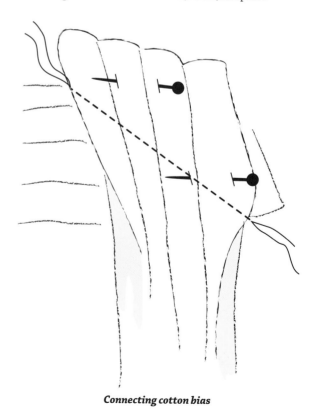

Connecting cotton bias

Finishing off cotton bias: When you're about to finish applying cotton bias, stop about 2" away from where your two ends come together. One edge should be stitched down, and the other end should have a loose "tail." The tail should extend 1" beyond the point it meets the other end of your trim. Tuck under ½" and let the additional ½" overlap the stitched side of the bias. Pin and stitch to finish.

Connecting Oilcloth Bias: For some projects you might need to make your 1" oilcloth bias strips longer. Do so by overlapping two strips with both strips right side up. Use your water soluble fabric marker to draw a 45° line and stitch the two pieces together along the line, making sure to backstitch at each end. Trim off the excess, leaving ⅛" on either side of the seam.

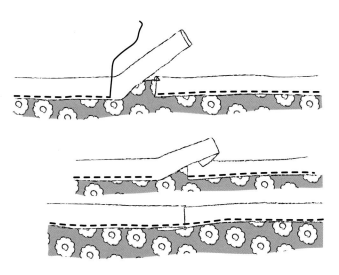

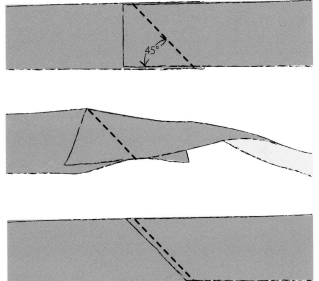

Connecting oilcloth bias

Cutting Oilcloth Bias: Lay your oilcloth face down on your work surface and use the 45° markers on your wide ruler to draw a diagonal line. Next use your ruler to mark 1" or 5" strips depending on the projects. Use the ruler and a rotary cutter to cut your bias strips.

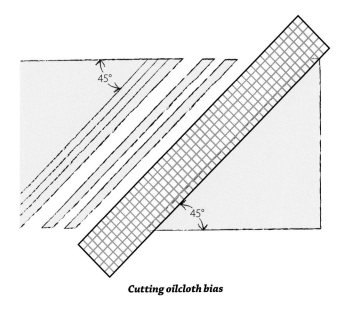

Cutting oilcloth bias

Faux Mitered Corner: When applying cotton bias tape or oilcloth bias trim to a project with corners, you need to create a faux mitered corner. Start by sandwiching the edge of the project within the bias, edge stitching the trim in place all the way to the end of the corner, and backstitching. Remove the piece from your machine and clip the threads. Fold open your bias and tuck the bottom half of the trim under the oilcloth to create a 45° angle with the top half of the trim. Now close the fold to encase the project within the trim, making sure your corners match up and create a tidy 45° angle. Pin and edge stitch.

Creating a faux mitered corner

Finishing Oilcloth Bias Trim: When you're about to finish applying oilcloth bias, stop about 2" away from where your two ends come together. One edge should be stitched down and the other end should have a loose "tail." The tail should extend ½" beyond the point where it meets the other end of trim. Cut the end on a slight diagonal. Layer the ½" over the stitched side of the bias, pin, and stitch to finish.

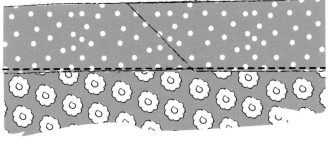

Finishing oilcloth bias trim

2

For the House

Simple Tablecloth

Simple Tablecloth

Finished Dimensions: 58" (W) × 78" (L) (finished size is customizable)

These days, tables don't seem to come in standard sizes, and it's impossible to find just the right size tablecloth in just the right color. This tablecloth pattern will help you through the process of creating a custom, one-of-a-kind oilcloth tablecloth. Oilcloth is perfect for an everyday tablecloth; just wipe it down with a damp cloth as needed. The following pattern walks you through the step-by-step process of piecing several panels of narrow oilcloth into a wide tablecloth.

June Suggests: Don't be afraid to play with color or patterns. There are so many great oilcloths out there, just have fun. This project would be great for laminated cotton instead of oilcloth.

Materials

5 yards of 47"/48" oilcloth for the body (see note regarding yardage)

1 1/2 yards of 47"/48" oilcloth for the trim (see note regarding yardage)

Matching thread for the trim

Wide clear ruler or T-square

Measuring tape

Pencil

Note: The yardage provided in the materials list is the amount that it took to make the sample tablecloth pictured and explained in the following pattern. Follow Steps 1 through 4 to find out how much yardage you need for your own special tablecloth.

Mark It Up and Cut It Out

1. The following steps help you estimate the yardage needed for your custom tablecloth. They also help you make a one-of-a-kind pattern. Start by measuring your tabletop's width and length. Make note of each of the measurements.

2. Decide on the drop of your tablecloth. Drop is the amount of the tablecloth that hangs over all the edges of the table. It's best for the drop to be equal on all four sides of the table. I prefer an 8" drop, but you might need it to be longer or shorter depending on your table and lifestyle. A family with young children might find a shorter drop more child-friendly, whereas a home that has a more traditional decor might demand the look of a longer drop. Be sure to make note of the measurements so you can figure out how much fabric you need.

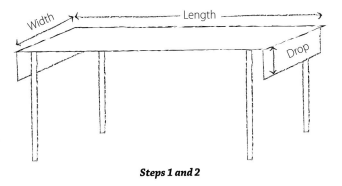

Steps 1 and 2

3. Because the drop is on all sides of the table, you need to multiply the drop by 2 and add this measurement to both the width and length. Plug your measurements into the following formula to help you find the finished measurements for your tablecloth. For example, for a table measuring 42" (W) × 62" (L) and a drop (D) of 8" on the tablecloth, the finished measurements are 58" wide and 78" long.

___" (D) × 2 = ___" + ___" (W) = ___" finished width of tablecloth

___" (D) × 2 = ___" + ___" (L) = ___" finished length of tablecloth

Note: Because oilcloth only comes in 47"/48" widths, you need to piece the oilcloth together to make sure that your tablecloth is wide enough to include the proper drop. To do so you need to add a length of fabric to each side of a center panel of oilcloth.

4. Now that you know the finished width and length of your tablecloth you can calculate the yardage required to make your custom tablecloth. If your tablecloth's finished width is more than 47"/48" wide, you need to add side panels to make the tablecloth wide enough to cover the table and have a drop. In order to have enough fabric, you need to buy yardage that equals twice the finished length of your tablecloth.

Continuing the example in Step 3, the tablecloth will be 58" wide and 78" long, so I need to add side panels for the tablecloth to cover the table nicely. That means I need to double the length of the table, which results in 156".

__" finished length of tablecloth × 2 = ___" (amount fabric needed)

Fabric is sold by the yard so it's best to convert inches to yards by dividing by 36".

___" (amount fabric needed) ÷ 36" = ___ yards

Note: Many oilcloth prints that have a fruit, flower, or lace motif have a pattern that repeats. If the oilcloth print that you picked has a notable repeat and you want to match it seamlessly, I suggest buying an extra ½ yard of fabric. Check to see what the repeat is on your chosen fabric before having it cut to size. You might find you need more or less fabric. For information on working with repeating prints, see page 8.

To know how big to make the panels for your tablecloth, you need to do a bit more math. Work out the following formulas on a piece of paper so you can transfer them directly onto the back of your oilcloth.

5. Determine the width of your center panel by adding 3" to the width of your tabletop. In my example, the table is 42" wide, so when I add the extra 3" I determine that I need my center panel to be 45" wide. Here it is written as a formula:

___" (W) + 3" = ___" width of center panel

Note: This formula includes two ½" seam allowances and an extra 1" on both sides of your table.

The exact measurement for the center panel is the width determined by this formula by the finished length of the tablecloth (refer to Step 3). My center panel measures 45" wide by 78" long.

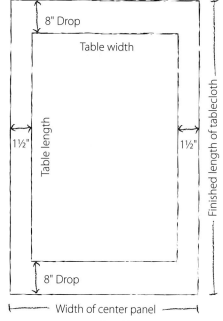

Step 5

6. To determine the width of the two lengths of fabric needed to achieve the full width of the tablecloth, simply subtract 1" from the drop length you determined in Step 2.

___" (drop) – 1" = ___" (width of one side panel)

In my example, I am using an 8" drop, so each of my two side panels needs to be 7" wide.

The side panels run the full length of your finished tablecloth, so the length you need for them is the same as the length of the center panel. For my tablecloth, I cut my side panels 7" wide by 78" long.

7. Now it's time to transfer the calculations onto the back of your oilcloth. With your ruler, measuring tape, and pencil (learn more about writing utensils and oilcloth on page 7) mark off the width and length for the center panel. Use your wide ruler or square to ensure your corners are square. Double-check your work and then cut out the center panel. Remember that we included seam allowances in our calculations, so you don't need to add any extra now.

8. Measure the width and length of side panels and mark them on to your oilcloth. Using the selvage edges of the oilcloth cuts down on cutting time. If you are matching up the pattern on your oilcloth, read about matching prints on page 8 in the tip section. Cut out your side panels.

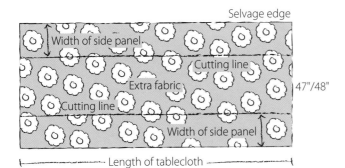

9. Cut enough 4" strips to trim for the perimeter of your tablecloth. It's fun to cut your trim on the bias, depending on your print. Cutting on the bias works well if you're using a print like a gingham or lace. If you're using a floral or a polka dot, it's not necessary to cut on the bias. (See page 11 for instructions on cutting oilcloth strips for trim.)

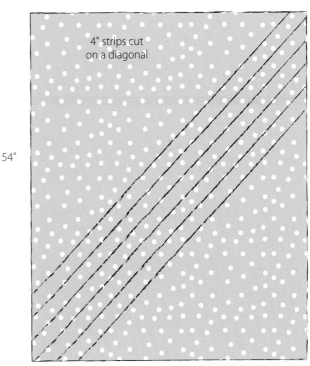

Step 8

Note: When cutting your trim it's best to use a rotary cutter to avoid jagged cutting lines that can happen when you use scissors.

Steps

1. Place one of the long sides of your center panel up to the selvage edge of a side panel with the right sides together and pin. (See page 7 for important information on pinning oilcloth.) If you are trying to match up a print, see page 8 in the tip section for more information. Also pin the second panel to the opposite side of the center panel.

2. Sew your side panels to your center panel using a ½" seam allowance.

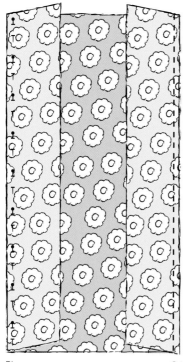

Pin

Stitch ½" on seam allowance

Steps 1 and 2

3. Lay your tablecloth on a flat work surface and unfold the side panels so that the right side of all three panels is facing up. Finger press all the seam allowances to the outside edges. (See page 9 for information on finger pressing.) There is no need to pin the seam in place; the oilcloth should behave and stay in place. Take the tablecloth back to the sewing machine and edge stitch each of the seam allowances into place against the side panels. Take the tablecloth back to the sewing machine and edge stitch each of the seam allowances into place against the side panels. This is a great time to use your fancy nonstick or roller foot. (See page 7 for information on presser feet.)

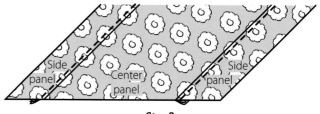

Step 3

4. Prep your 2" trim by sewing your strips into one long piece by overlapping the ends and edge stitching them in place. Page 11 has specific information on extending oilcloth trim.

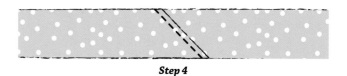

Step 4

5. After you're done stitching the trim together, use the edge of a table to crease press the trim in half. (See the pressing tips on page 9 for more information.) The crease helps you sew your trim onto the tablecloth.

6. Sandwich your folded trim around the edge of the tablecloth and pin along the inside edge of the trim, making sure to catch all three layers of trim and tablecloth with your pin. At the corners make a faux mitered corner (see page 12 to learn how to make the faux mitered corners). To finish off your oilcloth trim, overlap the ends ½". See page 13 for more details. After your trim is securely pinned, edge stitch your trim.

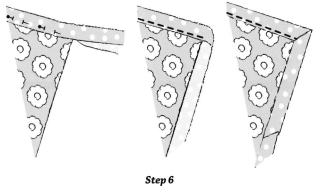

Step 6

7. Now you're ready to set the table for dinner! Remember oilcloth is great for every day, holiday, and outdoor dining. So you just might need to make a few more tablecloths again soon.

Chalk Cloth Table Runner

Chalk Cloth Table Runner

Finished Dimensions: 15" (W) × 77" (L)

This chalk cloth table runner is one of my most treasured possessions. I don't think I can have a party or holiday meal without one. It's a fun way to label party food or to share a drink recipe at a cocktail party. When the parties are over you can use it to leave love notes or let the kids use it for hours of drawing fun. While you're making yours, take a few extra minutes and make an extra, because it makes a wonderful hostess gift.

> **June Suggests:** The best thing about making your own pattern is being able to customize it. You can easily make your pattern to suit the size you need by adding or subtracting a few scallops. This way you can have one runner for a small sideboard and another for an extra-long table.

Materials

2¼ yards of 47"/48" chalk cloth
Craft paper for making your pattern
Card stock for tracing pattern pieces
Clear wide ruler or square
Pen or fine point marker

Steps

1. To create your table runner pattern, start with a rectangle of craft paper that measures 15" × 39½". Use a clear ruler or square to make sure that your corners are square.

2. Draw a line ¾" away from one of the 15" ends of the pattern to indicate the end of your runner.

3. On this same end of the paper, mark the center of the pattern by drawing a 5" line perpendicular to the center of the side (7½" from the long edge).

4. Draw lines parallel to each of the long sides of the paper; they should be 1¼" away from both of the 39½" sides of the pattern.

Steps 1 through 4

5. Copy pattern pieces A, B, and C from pages 124–126 onto card stock and cut out each pattern. Make sure to transfer the lines marked on the patterns in the book to your card stock patterns.

6. Place Piece A in the lower-right corner of your pattern paper, making sure to match the lines on the pattern pieces with the lines that you drew onto your pattern paper. Trace the circle.

7. Repeat Step 6 on the upper-right corner.

Steps 6 and 7

8. Place Piece B in the middle of the two circles you traced by matching the line on the pattern piece to the 5" line on your pattern paper. Trace the circle.

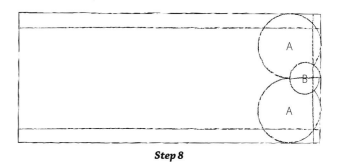

Step 8

9. Position Piece C on the line that is 1¼" from one of the long edges. Match the line on the pattern with the line on the paper. The end of the line should be touching the circle you drew from pattern piece A. Trace around the bottom portion of Piece C. Repeat to create the line of scallops along the long edges of the runner by matching the line on Piece C to the long line and the end of the previous scallop. Six scallops should fit along the edge.

Step 9

10. To ensure that your scallops are equally proportioned on both sides of your pattern, place a clear ruler across your pattern so that it is perpendicular to the long scalloped edge. The long edge of the ruler should be at the point where your first two scallops meet. Draw a line across the pattern paper.

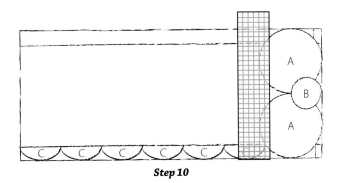

Step 10

11. Repeat, moving right to left until you have six lines.

12. Using the perpendicular lines as your guide, repeat Step 9 to draw the scallops along the opposite side of the pattern paper.

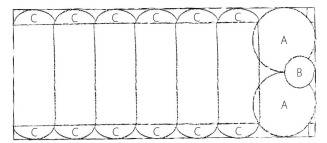

Steps 11 and 12

13. Cut around the edges of your paper pattern by following the lines you drew for the scallops along the edges.

14. Trace ½ of your chalk cloth table runner on the wrong side of an 80" long piece of chalk cloth. (To learn the best way to mark a pattern on to chalk cloth, see page 7.)

15. Flip the pattern over to the unmarked half of your chalk cloth and mark the second half.

Note: I find it helpful to use a yardstick to keep the table runner straight. Otherwise, it's easy to end up with a runner with an odd angle.

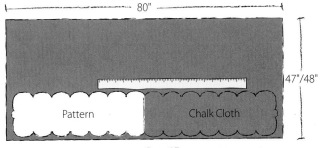

Step 15

16. Follow the lines you traced to cut out your scalloped table runner.

Note: Before using your fun chalk cloth runner, consider treating your chalk cloth. (See page 8 for tips on curing chalk cloth.)

17. Now you're all set to host a swanky party, so grab some chalk and get to scribbling!

Storage Bins

Finished Dimensions: Small Storage Bin: 6" (W) × 10½" (L) × 6¾" (H)
Medium Storage Bin: 7½" (W) × 12" (L) × 7¼" (H)
Large Storage Bin: 9" (W) × 13½" (L) × 8" (H)

Don't we all long to have a place for everything and everything in its place? Well, you can sew yourself toward that goal. You're going to want a million of these storage bins; they're great in every room in the house, from the craft room to the pantry. They hold everything from your bathroom towels to all that kid stuff in the mud room. With so many fun oilcloth prints to choose from, you can easily coordinate with your decor. You'll be so fashionably organized!

> June Suggests: Play with your patterns to make the bins bigger or smaller. You can also change the shape by changing the size of your pattern. For example, if you want a large square bin, make the bottom 14" (L) × 14" (W) instead of 14" (L) × 9½" (W).

Materials

2 yards of 47"/48" oilcloth for the exterior of a set of three storage bins (¾ yard for a single small or medium bin, 1 yard for a single large bin)

2¾ yards of 47"/48" oilcloth for the lining and interfacing for a set of three storage bins (1½ yard for a single small or medium bin, 1⅝ yard for a single large bin)

¼ yard of 47"/48" oilcloth for 1" oilcloth trim

1 fat quarter of chalk cloth (for optional labels)

1½ yards of 1"-wide nylon webbing to use as handles

1 to 2 spools of coordinating thread

Roll of craft paper

Double-sided tape

Clear ruler

Lighter

Mark It Up and Cut It Out

1. Making the pattern for the storage bins is easy; it's just a matter of putting a few simple shapes together. So grab your clear ruler and some craft paper and then get to work!

2. For the smallest of the three start by tracing a 6¼" × 11" rectangle onto your craft paper. This is the bottom of your bin. Next add two 6¼" × 11" rectangles to the top and the bottom of the first rectangle. Then, add two smaller squares, 6¼" × 6¼" on the right and the left of the first rectangle. These four shapes create the side walls for your small bin. Label this pattern as Piece A.

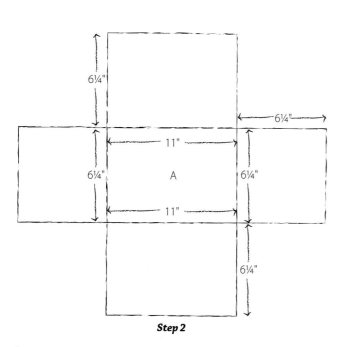

Step 2

4. Continue the process to make the largest bin pattern. The pattern starts with a 9½" × 14" rectangle for the bottom of the bin. The top and bottom rectangles are 7¼" × 14" and the sides are 7¼" × 9½". Label this pattern as Piece C.

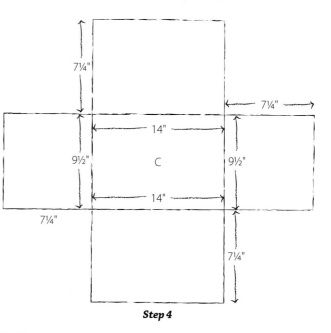

Step 4

3. Repeat the same process to make the pattern for the medium bin. Start with an 8" × 12½" rectangle. Add two 6¾" × 12½" rectangles to the top and bottom and two 6¾" × 8" rectangles to the left and right sides of the medium bin bottom. Label this pattern as Piece B.

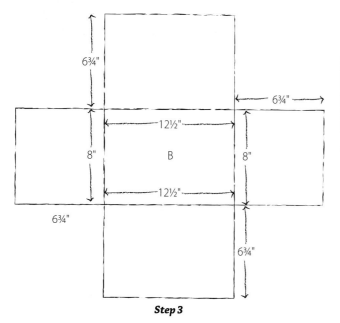

Step 3

5. Use your patterns to trace the pieces for each bin as described in the following table.

Oilcloth print	Piece A	Piece B	Piece C
#1	Cut 1	Cut 1	Cut 1
#2	Cut 2	Cut 2	Cut 2

6. Cut strips of Oilcloth Print #3 for trimming the bins.

- Cut 1 1" × 34" strip for trimming the small bin.
- Cut 1 1" × 40" strip for trimming the medium bin.
- Cut 1 1" × 46" strip for trimming the large bin.

7. Cut the handles for each bin. 1" webbing is a great time saver. Cut six 10" pieces of webbing.

8. If you're adding chalk cloth labels to your bins, cut out three 3" × 4" rectangles from your chalk cloth fat quarter.

Steps

1. Flat line the interfacing and lining pieces. See page 10 for information on how to flat-line your fabrics. Baste the interfacing and lining together using a ⅛" seam allowance. Set this aside while you prep the exterior of your bin.

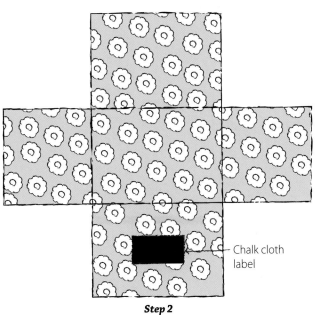

Step 2

3. Starting with the lining piece that you set aside in Step 1 fold each of the four side walls up and pin so that the right sides are together and make an open-topped box. Do the same with the exterior piece.

4. Sew all the corner edges together using a ¼" seam allowance. Make sure to backstitch at the beginning and end of each stitch line. After you have all the corners completed clip the bottom corners at an angle, being careful not to clip into your stitches.

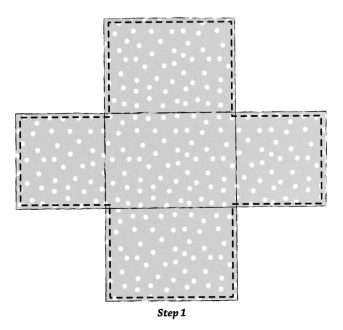

Step 1

2. Optional: Place your exterior piece right side up on your work surface and use double-sided tape to adhere the 3" × 4" chalk cloth label onto the center of one side of your bin. (It doesn't matter which side you place the label on; think about where you're going to use the bin and let that determine the ideal placement.) Use the clear ruler to ensure that your label is centered on the panel. Edge stitch the chalk cloth label into place. (See page 9 for information on edge stitching.)

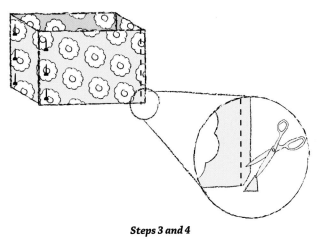

Steps 3 and 4

5. Turn the exterior right side out and slip the corresponding lining down into the exterior shell of the bin. The trick to getting nice-looking corners is to make the seam allowances of the lining shift to one direction and the seam allowances of the exterior to shift to the opposite direction. Aligning the seam allowances this way decreases bulk. Pin the exterior and lining pieces at the corners and along the top edge of your bin and then baste all the layers together using a ¼" seam allowance.

6. Prep the webbing handle pieces by melting the ends with a lighter. Do so by briefly running the flame of the lighter along each cut end of the webbing. This won't take long; you don't want the webbing to shrink and curl. You just want the ends to become shiny and slightly melted so that the webbing doesn't fray out.

Note: Please be cautious when melting the nylon. Keep it away from your skin and only do this in a well-ventilated area.

7. Determine the center of the top edge of the narrow side of your bin and mark it by placing a pin perpendicular to the top edge. Position the handles 1¼" off to the left and right of the center pin. Pin the webbing in place and zigzag-stitch the handles to the top edge of the bin.

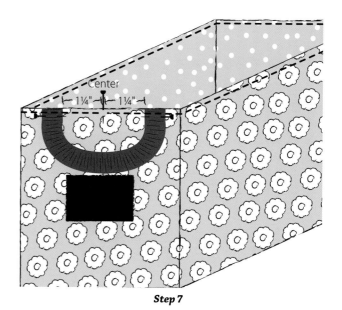

Step 7

8. Crease press a fold (see page 9 for information on crease pressing) into your strips of 1" trim. Starting about 2" from one corner, sandwich the top edge of the storage bin into your folded trim and pin the trim in place, making sure to pin along the stitch line. When you get to the place where the two ends of your trim meet, overlap the end of the trim about ¾" over the start of the trim.

10. Flip the handles upward and pin them in place. Stitch the webbing to the trim along the same stitch line used for the trim. (You might need to change the top thread to match the handle.) For added strength, stitch the handles twice.

11. Repeat these steps for the other two bins.

12. Now you're ready to get organized. Just fill the bins and use the chalk cloth label to identify the contents!

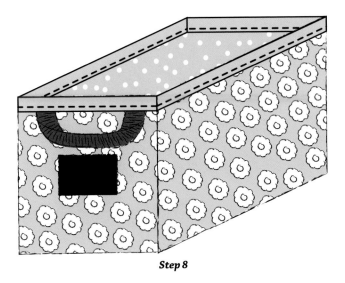

Step 8

9. Edge stitch the trim in place. (See page 9 for information on edge stitching.) It is helpful to remove the extension table from your sewing machine when stitching the trim of this project in place. Working with the free arm makes all the difference. Stitching the trim on is a slow process. As you work your way around the top edge of the bin don't fret when you need to flatten out the corners; the oilcloth is firm enough to stand up again when you're done stitching.

Step 10

Chalk Cloth Labels

Chalk Cloth Labels

Finished Dimensions: 5" diameter

Here's a project to use up all those oilcloth scraps left over from all the great projects that you have been working on. This pattern was originally intended to be a simple hanging label to help keep you organized, but with a little playing around it became much more. Add a longer trim and you can wrap a package, or just leave the trim off and you have a super cute coaster.

> June suggests: Go crazy with the trims and use what you have; this is a great way to de-stash. Use ribbon, rickrack, a funky yarn, or heavy string as ties for your one-of-a-kind tags.

Materials

1 fat quarter of chalk cloth (18" × 22")

1 to 3 fat quarters of oilcloth (18" × 22" each)

Double-stick tape

Ribbon and/or rickrack

Coordinating thread

Pinking shears (optional)

Mark It Up and Cut It Out

1. Photocopy Patterns A, B, and C from pages 127–129.

2. Use Pattern A to trace and cut a circle from the chalk cloth.

3. Trace Pattern B on to oilcloth and then use pinking shears or regular scissors to cut it out.

4. Trace Pattern C on two different oilcloth prints and cut out the flower shapes.

Steps

1. Tape the chalk cloth and oilcloth circles together with double-stick tape. The wrong side of the chalk cloth should be facing the right side of the oilcloth. Sew them together by edge stitching close to the perimeter of the oilcloth circle. (See the edge stitch tip on page 9.)

Step 1

2. Place the two flower pieces together, wrong sides facing. You can align the edges or stagger the pieces for a dimensional effect. Tape the layers together in the center.

3. Take a 12" ribbon (or whatever you're using for your ties) and fold it in half to create your ties for the tag. Sandwich the ribbon between the two flower layers of the label. Do so by opening the two flowers on one side and then taping the ribbon 1" away from the outside edge of the flower.

Step 3

4. After you have your ties in place, center your chalk and oilcloth circles on to the right side of your flower and tape them into place. The chalk cloth circle should be face up and on the topmost layer. Edge stitch all four pieces together on the inside edge of the oilcloth circle.

5. Enjoy getting organized with your fun new reusable Chalk Cloth Labels!

Garden Apron

Garden Apron

Finished Dimensions: Sample shown is 12" long with an 18" waist and 28" apron strings (fits woman size 4–14)

This super sweet apron is great for the garden or in the craft room. There are plenty of pockets to keep your tools close at hand. What gardener wouldn't love this for a gift?

June Suggests: To change up this apron a bit, go with one print or, for some quirky fun, make each pattern piece of the apron a different fabric pattern.

Materials

$\frac{1}{2}$ yard of 47"/48" oilcloth for small pocket (Piece A) and trim (Piece F)

$\frac{1}{2}$ yard of 47"/48" oilcloth for pleated pocket section (Piece B) and large pocket section (Piece C)

$\frac{1}{2}$ yard of 47"/48" oilcloth for apron front (Piece D) and the smaller trim (Piece E)

1 or 2 spools of coordinating thread

1 package of $\frac{1}{2}$" double-fold bias tape

Wide clear ruler or square

Craft paper

Pencil

Tracing paper and smooth edge tracing wheel

Press-on snaps

Mark It Up and Cut It Out

1. The pattern for this apron is just a series of rectangles, so grab some craft paper, ruler, and a pencil and make the pattern.

Note: Mark the patterns with the correct letter and note how many pieces need to be cut for quick reference when it comes to cutting your fabric pieces out.

Measure and cut out the pattern pieces using the following table.

Note: E–H can be marked and cut directly on your fabric.

Pattern A	4" × 11" small pocket, cut 1
Pattern B	6" × 28" long pleated pocket, cut 1
Pattern C	8" × 20" large double pocket, cut 1
Pattern D	12" × 20" apron, cut 1
Pattern E	1" × 12" oilcloth trim for Pocket A, cut 1
Pattern F	1" × 22" oilcloth trim for Pocket C, cut 1
Pattern G	1" × 30" oilcloth trim for Pocket B, cut 1
Pattern H	1" × 47" oilcloth trim for side and bottom apron edges

2. Mark the stitch lines and/or darts on Patterns A through D according to the following directions and illustrations.

Pattern A: Mark the center of the 11" side of the pattern with a notch, dividing it in half horizontally. Notches are little triangle marks along the bottom edge of the pattern.

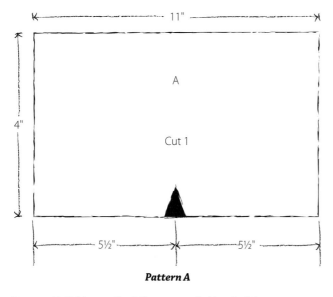

Pattern A

Pattern B: Fold your 6" × 28" pattern in half to find the center, open the paper, and draw a 4" stitch line in the crease, starting at the bottom edge of the paper.

Pattern B: The next step is to mark notches on the bottom edge of the pattern to indicate the positions of the pocket pleat folds. Mark the first notch 4½" to the left of the center stitch line. Mark the second notch 1" to the left of the first notch. Mark the third notch 5" to the left of the second notch. Mark the fourth notch 1" to the left of the third notch. Repeat the marking process on the right side of the pattern. You should end up with eight notches total, spaced as shown in the illustration.

Pattern B: Mark a dot 4½" in from the 6" side of the pattern and 4½" up from the bottom of the pattern to indicate the snap placement. Mark a second dot from the other 6" side using the same measurements.

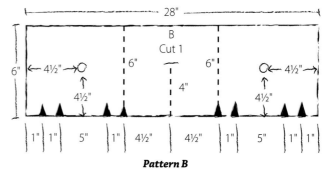

Pattern B

Pattern C: Mark a dot 2½" away from one of the 8" sides of the pattern and 4½" up from the bottom. Mark a second dot on the other side using the same measurements. These dots are for the second half of the snaps.

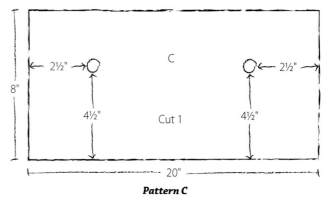

Pattern C

Pattern D: Draw an 8" stitch line down the center, dividing the pattern in half horizontally. This pattern gets two darts; start making the first dart by placing a small dot 5½" in from each 12" side and 4" down from the top. Next, place a small pencil line along the top edge of the pattern that is 5½" away from the 12" side. Connect this pencil line to your dot to indicate the dart's center. (See the illustration.) Next measure and mark ½" away from each side of the center line of the dart. Connect the dot with the two ½" marks as shown in the illustration. Fold Pattern D in half and mark the second dart on the other side as shown in stitch mark diagram.

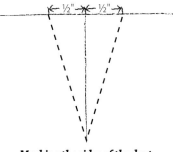

Marking the sides of the dart

3. Trace your pattern pieces on to your oilcloth. Use a pencil to write the letter of each piece on the wrong side of the fabric. Write the letter in the seam allowance.

4. Use your tracing paper and smooth edge wheel to transfer all stitch lines, notches, dots, and darts to the back of your fabric for Pieces A through D and then cut out your pieces.

Steps

1. Fold trim Pieces E, F, and G in half the long way and press to form a crease. Insert the top edge of Pieces A, B, and C into the folds of the pieces of trim and pin the trim to the pocket pieces. Leave ½" extending at both ends of the pocket to avoid having the trim get caught up in your machine's needle plate. Stitch along the edge of the trim and then cut the trim even with the edges of the pockets.

2. Place Piece A on top of Piece B, making sure to match the center notch on Piece A with the stitch line on the back of Piece B. Pin along the bottom of Piece A (making sure to pin about ⅛" from the bottom to avoid any pesky pin holes) and machine baste along the bottom and sides of the pocket.

3. On the wrong side of Piece B sew along the central stitch line. Be sure to backstitch at the top of the pocket as this will be a stress point. Attach the snap to Pieces B and C using the manufacturer's directions. The top snap half should be on Piece B with the working side on the wrong side of the material. The bottom snap half should be on Piece C with the working side on the right side of the material.

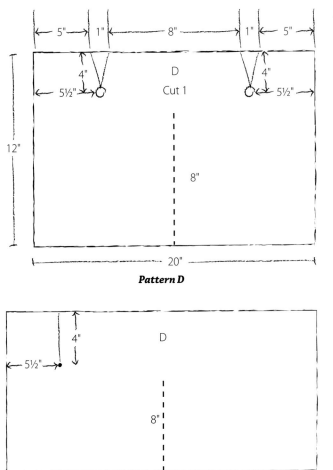

Pattern D

Marking the center line of the dart

4. Place Piece C on the apron front (Piece D) so that both of the right sides are facing up. Match up the sides and the bottom edges and pin them together along the very bottom as you did in Step 2. Flip the two pieces over so that the wrong side of the apron is facing up. Pin along the stitch line that you drew earlier on the back of the apron (Piece D) and stitch the pieces together. Leave the rest of Piece C loose for the time being.

5. Snap Piece B onto Piece C and pin the sides of all three pockets together along the edges. (See the illustration.) You do not pin the pockets to the apron at this time, so fold the apron to one side while you pin each side of the pockets together.

Step 6

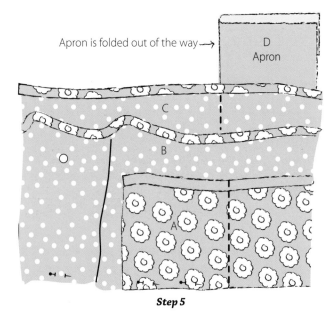

Step 5

6. It's important to keep the main apron layer off to the side while you're completing this step of creating the pleated pockets. Start with the outer pleats first. The folds will be at the positions of the notches, and the outer fold will end up ½" from the edge. Put a pin in the corner to hold the pleat in place. (See the illustration.)

7. Next finger press the inner pleats. (See page 9 for information on finger pressing.) Again, the folds will be at the positions of the notches, but they will be the mirror image of the outer folds. Open the pleat that is closest to the center and insert a pin on the inside of that pleat. (See the illustration.)

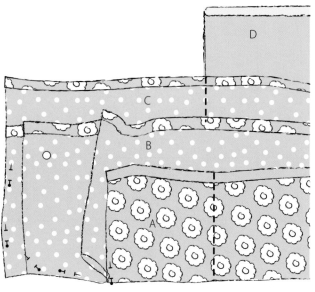

Step 7

8. Leave the pleat open and use your clear ruler to make the next stitch line. Place the ¾" line of the ruler along the innermost fold crease of the pleat and mark a stitch line with a few pins. (See the illustration.)

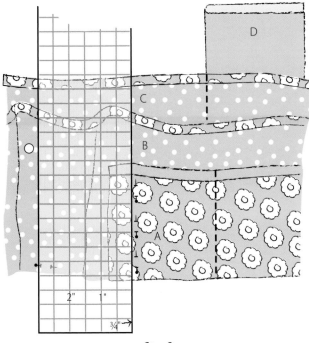

Step 8

9. Topstitch the side pockets by following the pin line. Refold the inner pleats and pin them into place along the bottom.

10. Unfold the apron and place it and the pockets flat on your work surface and pin the outer edges of the pocket to the apron before basting them together. Sew the darts into the top of the apron and then finger press the darts to the outer sides before basting along the top.

11. Using trim Piece H, start at the top right side of the apron and leave ½" of extra trim above the top edge so that the trim doesn't get caught in your machine's needle plate. To avoid pinholes, pin along the stitch line. At each corner, pleat the trim into a faux mitered corner as described on page 12.

12. Use the ½" cotton bias tape to create your apron strings and to bind of top of the apron. Fold in one end of the bias ½" and pin the end.

13. Measure 28" from the end of the bias. At that point, start pinning the bias across the apron. When you reach the opposite edge of the apron, measure another 28", cut the bias, and fold both ends of the bias ½" and pin.

14. Edge stitch the bias to the apron top and stitch the folded ends of the apron strings. (See page 9 for tips on edge stitching bias.)

15. Now it's time to load up your fancy new apron with tools and go get dirty, but don't worry. The apron will just wipe clean with a damp towel!

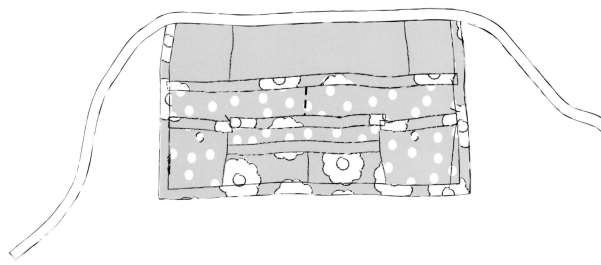

Step 14

Seat Cushions

Seat Cushions

Finished Dimensions: Bottom Cushion: 4" (D) × 22" (W) × 44" (L)
Back Cushion: 4" (D) × 17" (W) × 44" L

Rain or shine, custom-made seat cushions in weather-friendly and easy-to-clean oilcloth won't let you down. Oilcloth fades in full sun, so be sure to use these seat cushions in a shady spot or on a covered porch. You'll find that an oilcloth cushion is great for window seats and the family banquet! For this pattern I walk you through how to make a custom pattern for your special project. Along the way, I give you specifics on the boxed cushions made for my cute vintage settee that will adorn my front porch for years to come.

> June Suggests: Get really fancy and add piping to your seams for added contrast. I suggest using cotton or heavy-weight nylon for the piping, as oilcloth is not the right fabric for the job.

Materials

1⅓ yards of 47"/48" oilcloth for the top layer of each seat cushion

1⅓ yards of 47"/48" oilcloth for the reverse side of each seat cushion

1⅓ yards of 47"/48" oilcloth for the welt piece of the seat cushion

2½ yards of 4" high-density foam

16 heavy-duty snaps

Electric carving knife or serrated knife

Wide ruler

Tracing paper

Craft paper

Smooth edge tracing wheel

Note: If you are using a fabric with a strong pattern, such as the lace print or a floral, you should buy extra to account for the pattern's repeat. (See page 8 for more information on matching patterns.)

Mark It Up and Cut It Out

1. On the inside of the seat, measure the width, length, and height. If you are adding a back cushion, the height is the height of the seat back minus the thickness of the bottom cushion, which is the thickness of the foam you have chosen (in my case it is 4" in depth). The settee that is pictured is 22" wide, 44" long, and 21" high.

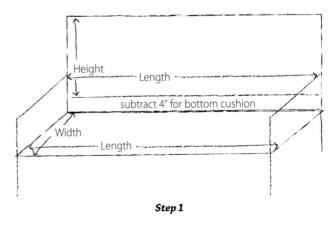

Step 1

2. Take the measurements from Step 1 and add ½" and then mark the cutting lines on to the foam. This extra ½" of foam fills out the finished cushion cover nicely to make it nice and taut. Mark the cutting lines on both sides of the foam. For example, my settee bottom measured 22" wide × 44" long so I cut the foam 22½" × 44½".

As for the back cushion, after I subtracted the depth (4") of the bottom cushion and added the extra ½", the back measured 17½" high and 44½" long.

3. Place your foam flat on a work table with the end you are cutting hanging over the table's edge, and use an electric carving knife or a serrated knife to cut the foam. Guide your knife slowly and carefully through the lines. I found it very helpful to flip the cushion over every few inches so I could make sure that I was cutting a straight and perpendicular line.

4. Check the foam pieces on the settee and make any necessary adjustments to the foam before making your paper pattern.

5. Mark the length and width of the bottom seat cushion on a large piece of craft paper and then add twice the thickness of your foam (in my case 4" × 2" = 8") to the width to create the back flap/closure of the cushion cover. Also add ½" to all four sides of your pattern for the seam allowances. Mark this as Piece A. For my sample, Piece A measures 31" (W) × 45" (L).

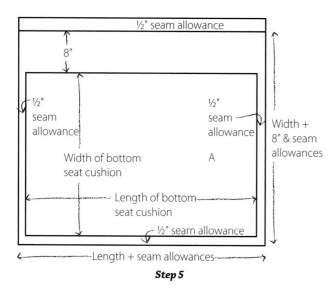

Step 5

6. The side welts are the panels of fabric that give a box cushion its depth. Make the side welt pattern by drawing the width of the cushion by the depth of the cushion (in my case 4"), on to a second piece of craft paper (label it Piece B). What you have just drawn will be your stitch lines that you will transfer to your oilcloth in a later step; having stitch lines is important when making box cushions. You'll need them to guide you when you sew the project together. Extend the pattern twice the thickness of your foam (in my case 8") to the width of Piece B. Again, add ½" to all edges for seams for your seam allowance. The final width of Piece B should be the same as the width of Piece A. The measurements of my sample's Piece B is 31" (W) × 5" (D).

7. Make the front welt pattern on a third sheet of craft paper by marking the length of the cushion by the required depth (4"). Add ½" seam allowances to all four edges (label this Piece C). You use Piece C for both the bottom and the back cushions, if applicable. For my sample, Piece C is 45" (L) × 5" (D). Note: The length should be the same as that of Piece A, and the depth should be the same as that of Piece B.

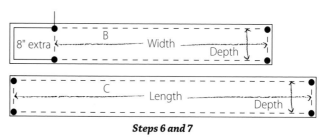

Steps 6 and 7

8. Take a moment to check your paper patterns against the foam to ensure your measurements are correct. Remember that your pattern has ½" seam allowances and an additional 8" for the back flap/closure. Make any necessary adjustments.

9. Use the length of your settee, chair, or bench to find out how much fabric to buy. Again, my settee was 44" wide so I needed 1⅓ yards of the three different oilcloths. See page 8 for more information on matching prints.

10. Use your custom patterns to cut the seat cushion cover pieces. On the wrong side of the cloth, label each piece of fabric with the same letter as the pattern piece you used to create it. Cut two of Piece A, two of Piece B, and one of Piece C.

11. Use tracing paper and a smooth edge tracing wheel to transfer the stitch lines to your oilcloth. Make a dot where the ½" seam allowances meet in each corner.

Note: It's important that you mark your stitch lines and dots onto the oilcloth on all the welt pieces (B and C).

Steps

1. Start off by constructing the welt for the cushion. Place Piece C on your work surface with the right side up. Lay one Piece B on top with the right side down, aligning its short end with the short end of Piece C. Be sure that you are pinning the end without the extra 8" to Piece C; you need to match the dots on the pieces. Do the same thing with the second Piece B on the opposite end of Piece C. Pin the ends of the strips and then sew from dot to dot using your ½" stitch line, making sure to leave ½" free at the top and bottom of each seam. Backstitch at each dot.

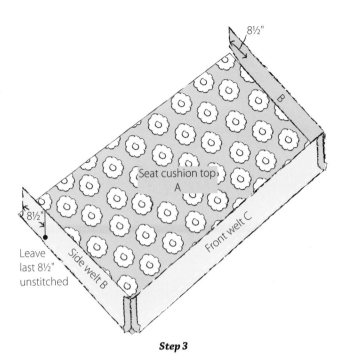

Step 3

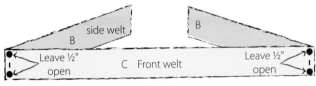

Step 1

2. Pin the front welt (Piece C) to a cushion Piece A with the right sides together, and sew from dot to dot using your stitch line as a guide. Backstitch at each dot. Again you should leave ½" unstitched at each end.

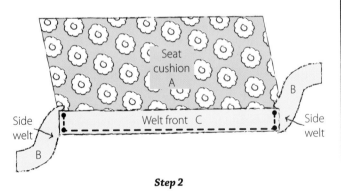

Step 2

3. Pin the side welts (Pieces B) to the sides of the seat cushion (Piece A), making sure that you have the front welt and seat cushion out of the way. Again, sew from dot to dot along the ½" stitch line. The extension (twice the foam thickness plus ½", in my case 8½") at the back remains open.

4. Crease press the welt seams open and repeat Steps 2 and 3 to attach the second cushion Piece A. (See page 9 for information on crease pressing.) When you're finished, you'll have an open-sided box for your seat cushion.

5. Now lay the cushion cover flat on to a table with the open end of the box cushion cover closest to you. Use a ruler and pencil to mark a fold line on Piece A near the two side welts. Make the mark that is the foam thickness away from your stitch lines where Piece A is sewn to Piece B. This line is your fold line for the closure. If you are using 2"-thick foam then your fold line is 2" from your stitch line. My foam is 4", thus my fold line is 4" from the stitch line. Flip the cushion cover over and mark the second Piece A the same way.

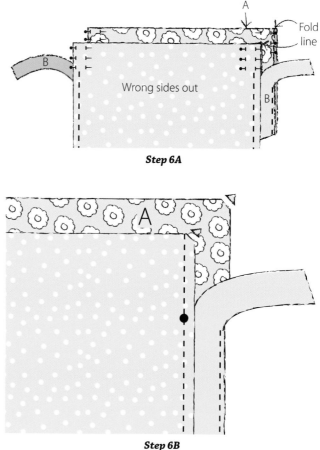

Step 6A

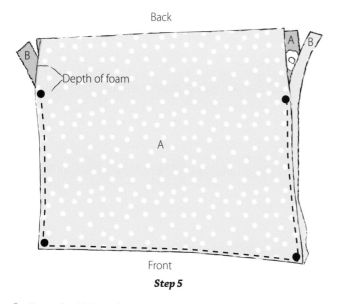

Step 5

6. Using the fold line that you created in Step 5 as your guide, fold the back closure flap on one Piece A over so that the right sides are together. Now pin this small flap closed on both sides of Piece A. (See the illustration for Step 6A.) With the side welts out of the way, stitch from the fold to the dot/stitch line, ½" from the aligned edges. Clip your corners at the fold as shown in the illustration for Step 6B.

Step 6B

7. Flip the back closure flaps so that the right side of the fabric is out and then lay the cushion on your work surface. Crease press both the top and bottom back flaps along the fold line and pin (clothespins are a great alternative for this application). Edge stitch near the fold line.

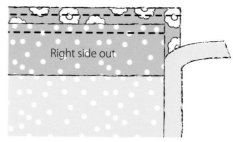

Step 7

8. Finish both of the side welt Pieces B by turning under a ½" hem and stitching the hem in place. These side welts will tuck up and under the seat cushion closure that you finish in the next step.

10. Repeat the pattern making process and assembly Steps 1 through 9 to make the back cushion, if applicable.

11. All that's left is to slide the foam inserts into your cushion covers and enjoy your comfy seat. So grab some iced tea and lounge!

Right sides out

Step 8

9. Turn the cushion cover right side out. Work the corners between your fingers to fully roll out the seams. Evenly space the top half of each snap along the back of the seat cushion, ⅝" away from the edge and with about 6" between the snaps. Apply the snaps according to the manufacturer's instructions; make sure to put the finished side of the snap on the outside flap. Place the opposite side of each snap 2⅜" away from the edge of the second flap. Be careful to align the snap halves so that the spacing is the same. After double-checking the spacing, apply the bottom half of the snap along the second flap.

Side welt

½"

Top flap

2⅜"   Bottom flap

Step 9

Party Banners

Party Banners

Finished Dimensions: 9' 27" (L)

Everyone loves a party, and these chalk and oilcloth party banners are sure to get the party started! Use the chalk cloth to make a statement like Happy Birthday or flip them to the oilcloth side for everyday use. There will be no more throwing away paper decorations because your new buntings will last for years and years! Beware, I find that they are best used in mass so be sure to make plenty for your next soirée. Don't forget your gift list; the banners make perfect gifts for all the party animals on your list.

June Suggests: Try different variations on different banners. Some things you could do include leaving out the chalk cloth to make an all-oilcloth banner or creating a color theme using one, two, or three different prints.

Materials

⅝ yard chalk cloth

⅝ yard oilcloth

4 yards (at least 2 packages—all one color or mix and match) of ½" double-fold bias tape for the banner edging

8 yards (at least 3 packages—all one color or mix and match) of ¼" double-fold bias tape for trimming the flags

Fine tip marker

Pencil

Card stock

Craft and fabric scissors

One spool of coordinating thread for each color of bias tape

Mark It Up and Cut It Out

1. Copy the pattern from page 136 onto card stock and then cut out the pattern using your craft scissors.

2. Using your pattern, trace 14 scalloped flag pieces onto the wrong side of the chalk cloth. It's hard to see pencil on the wrong side of the chalk cloth, so use a marker instead.

3. Trace 14 scalloped flag pieces on the wrong side of your oilcloth, but use a pencil because pen and marker bleed through oilcloth and can ruin a project.

4. Cut out your 14 chalk cloth and oilcloth scalloped flag pieces using your fabric scissors.

Note: You should make your banner to fit your needs. For example, 14 banners is enough for "Happy Birthday" with a space in between the two words. If you want to customize your banner to say "Happy Graduation" you need 16 scallops.

Steps

1. Pair a chalk cloth scallop with an oilcloth scallop and pin them together at the top. Place your pins close to the top edge so any pinholes will be covered with your ½" bias strings.

2. Sandwich the chalk cloth and oilcloth pairs within a 19" piece of the ¼" double-fold bias tape as seen in the illustration and pin the trim into place. Leave a ½" tab at each end of the flag to help keep your bias from jamming into the needle plate of your sewing machine when you begin and end each flag.

3. Set your sewing machine to 3.5, which is a nice stitch length for this project. I suggest using an open presser foot that has a ¼" opening (see the "Super H" foot tip on page 6) and then move your needle position to the next-to-last position on the left side. Center your pinned flags within the open part of the presser foot. The small bias fits in the ¼" opening of the foot nicely, and using the foot as your guide helps you achieve a nice even edge stitch.

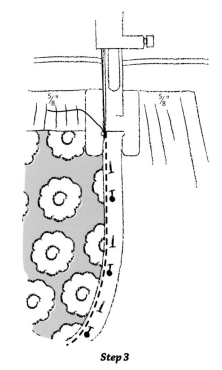

Step 3

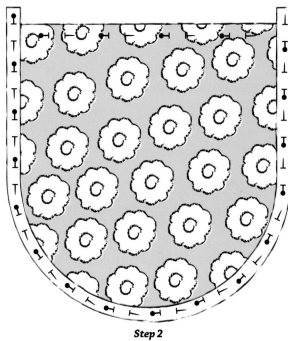

Step 2

Note: If you are comfortable trimming the flag without pinning, I suggest that you leave a ½" tab at the top, and sew the trim in place by sandwiching the trim as you edge stitch it into place. You can make quick work of trimming the scalloped flags by using the chain piecing method. Just leave a 1" to 2" space between each flag; Keep in mind that you need a bit more bias tape with this method.

4. Edge stitch the trim onto the scalloped flags. After you have applied trim to all of your flags cut the extra bias flush with the top of each scalloped flag.

5. Flip your scalloped flags over so you can see the oilcloth side and arrange your patterns to suit your taste. Stack them in order.

6. Use the ½" double-fold bias to create the string for each banner. If you are using pre-packaged bias tape from the fabric store, you need to piece two packages together to ensure that you have enough. (See page 10 for details on piecing bias together.) Cut the bias to a length of 9'27".

7. Finish off the first of the end of your string by turning in ½" of bias so that the raw end of the bias is neatly tucked inside the double fold. Pin into place. Now, place a second pin 18" away from the end of your bias string; this is the mark where you start adding the flags.

8. Edge stitch the tape closed until you get to the 18" mark, at which point you need to sandwich the first flag into the double-fold bias before continuing to edge stitch the bias. Butt the second flag up to the first one, continuing this process until you have sewn all 14 flags into the bias string.

9. You are now left with an extra 18" of bias beyond the final flag, which is your second end. Finish sewing the bias closed, making sure to tuck in the last ½" as you did in Step 7.

10. The last step is the best step: Just hang up your banners and invite everyone over for a fiesta!

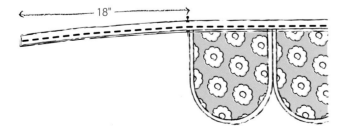

18"

Pillow Cover

Pillow Cover

Finished Dimensions: Pillow–16" square
Bee Appliqué–9½" × 9½"

When I start working out a new appliqué, I first come up with my theme and then I start looking at my oilcloth prints to find a shape or a small piece of oilcloth that fits into the appliqué. It's like creating a puzzle. The Paradise Lace Prints are the most intricate of all the oilcloths, and it's fun and easy to find a shape that works. For the bumblebee I studied old encyclopedia illustrations to get a feel for the size, shape, and scale needed to create an appliqué. To add depth to an appliqué, add a layer of a coordinating oilcloth behind the appliqué and cut it a bit larger than the original pattern.

June suggests: Mix it up! With so many great oilcloth prints to pick from you could make a hundred pillows and never make the same one twice. So add a couple of simple pillows in with your extra-special appliquéd pillow as well. You can also put the bee appliqué on things other than pillows, such as a tote, a picnic mat, or a tablecloth. (For more information and suggestions about appliquéing with oilcloth see page 10.)

Materials

Note: The prints listed are for duplicating the bee shown in the photograph. Feel free to make substitutions. For example, a fruit or floral print would make great wings, and a dot would work fine for the abdomen. The chalk cloth provides great dimension, but you could use a simple oilcloth print as an alternative.

½ yard of oilcloth for the main pillow front and back

¼ yard of lace oilcloth for the bee's antennae, head, thorax, and wings

½ yard gingham oilcloth for the bee's abdomen and the trim for the pillow

Fat quarter (or ⅛ yard) of chalk cloth for the bee's neck, wings, and thorax

Scrap of oilcloth to coordinate with gingham for the bee's neck (I used a solid yellow portion from a print)

1 package of medium rickrack to coordinate with oilcloth fabrics

Thread to coordinate with the back of pillow and bias

Water soluble fabric marker

Double-stick tape

16" pillow form

Mark It Up and Cut It Out

1. From your main oilcloth material, cut one 16" × 16" square for the pillow front and cut two 11" × 16" pieces for the pillow back. In my sample I chose a perky black polka dot oilcloth (but as I mentioned, you should feel free to mix it up).

2. Use the patterns on pages 130, 131, and 133 to trace Pieces A, B, D, and F of the bee on the lace oilcloth. You can see by the shapes where they should be positioned on the lace pattern. If you are using a different print, experiment with different placements to get just the right look. Trace the shapes using the water-soluble marker. Cut out the pieces after you've traced them. Wipe any ink off of your oilcloth before going on.

Note: The wings are made of four pieces of Piece F, which are mirrored in pairs on each side of the bee as shown in the illustration.

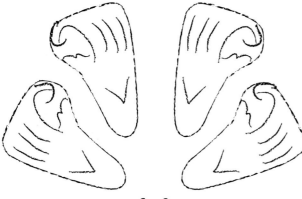

Step 2

3. Trace the pattern for the bee's neck, Pattern C from page 130, onto the back of the chalk cloth and the solid yellow scrap and then cut out the pieces.

4. Trace the pattern for the bee's abdomen, Pattern E from page 132, onto the back of the gingham and cut it out.

5. Trace two large wing patterns, Pattern G from page 134, onto the back of the chalk cloth creating two mirrored images.

6. Trace a large thorax, Pattern H from page 135, onto the back of the chalk cloth and cut it out.

7. Cut two 1" × 36" strips of oilcloth gingham to use as the pillow's trim. See page 7 for more information on cutting oilcloth.

Steps

1. Center the oilcloth head piece near the top of the larger chalk cloth neck piece as shown in the illustration and use double-stick tape to keep them together. Using black thread edge stitch the two together.

2. Place the chalk cloth neck piece onto the solid oilcloth neck piece, making sure to leave ¼" of solid color showing at the base of the chalk cloth neck. Use double-stick tape to keep the pieces together. Stitch the bottom of the chalk cloth neck to the second layer.

3. Use some tiny dots of double-stick tape to attach the antennae to your finished head. See the illustration.

Steps 1 through 3

4. Use double-stick tape to attach Piece D (the oilcloth thorax) to Piece H (the chalk cloth thorax). Stitch them together. (See the illustration.)

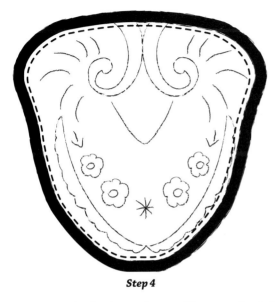

Step 4

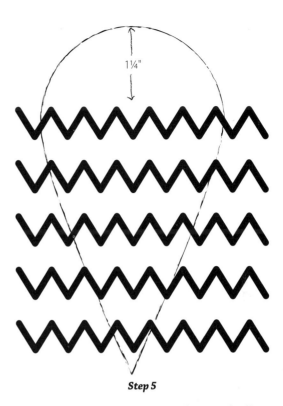

Step 5

5. Cut five pieces of rickrack: two that are 4" long, one that is 3⅝" long, another one that measures 2¾" long, and a fifth piece that is 2" long. Create stripes on the gingham abdomen by stitching five rows of rickrack along every other white stripe of the gingham. The top row of rickrack is approximately 1¼" away from the top edge of the abdomen. If you are working with a print other than gingham, make sure that your lines of rickrack are evenly spaced. Leave ½" of rickrack extending on either side of the abdomen as shown in the illustration.

6. Layer and tape your two wing pieces as shown in the illustration and use double-stick tape to keep them together.

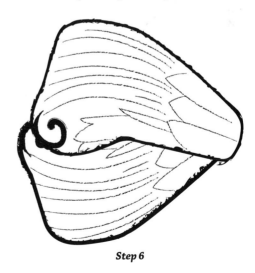

Step 6

7. Stick the bottom wing piece on to the chalk cloth, Piece G, first making sure it is about ⅛" from the bottom edge of the chalk cloth. Layer the top piece of the wing on top of the bottom piece, so that ⅛" is visible along the top edges as well. Repeat with the second set of wings and be sure to flip the wings to create a mirror image of the first set. Sew wings to Piece G.

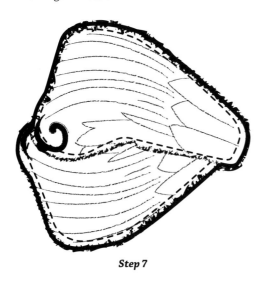

Step 7

8. Assemble the bee by layering the head over ⅞" of the top of the thorax, using double-stick tape to keep it in place. Then layer the thorax on top of the abdomen, overlapping 1", and tape. Lastly, tape the wings under the thorax. The thorax should overlap the tip of the wings by 1". You now have a cute little bumblebee to appliqué onto your pillow. (See the illustration.)

Tuck wing under 1"

Overlap head & neck ⅞"

Overlap thorax 1" onto abdomen

Tuck wing under 1"

Step 8

9. Place your bee on to the pillow front at an angle and use double-stick tape to keep it in place. The bottom tip of the abdomen should be about 1½" from the bottom left side edge and about 5" away from the left side of the pillow.

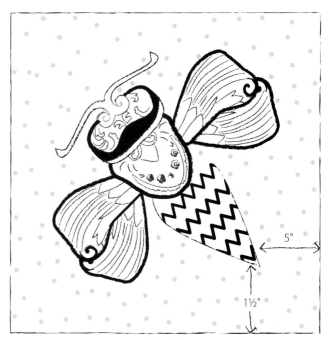

5"

1½"

Step 9

10. Using black thread, edge stitch the main sections to the pillow top. On the abdomen, turn the ½" ends of rickrack under the bee and stitch around the edges of the abdomen to secure it in place.

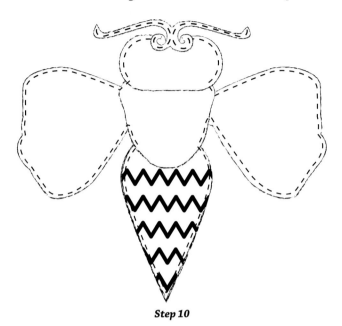

Step 10

11. Finish off the back pieces of the pillow by making a 1" fold over to the wrong side on one 16" edge of each pillow back piece. Edge stitch the folds into place.

12. Lay your 16" × 16" pillow front face down on a work surface. Then lay the two back pieces onto the pillow front with the right sides facing up. (In other words, the wrong sides are facing.) Match the raw edges of the pillow front and the two pillow backs so that they make a 16" square. The two pillow backs overlap 3" in the middle of the pillow. Pin the pillow front and pillow backs at the outer edges and then baste the pillow together using a ¼" seam allowance. *Tip*: Pin within the outer ¼" of the pillow to avoid pinholes in your pillow cover.

13. Fold your 1" strip of gingham oilcloth trim in half lengthwise and crease press. (See page 9 for tips on crease pressing and page 11 for lengthening oilcloth trim.)

14. To apply the trim, start pinning your trim about 1½" away from a corner. Sandwich the trim around the outer edges of the pillow cover and pin it in place. Pin along your stitch line to avoid pinholes. At each corner pleat the trim into a faux mitered corner. (See page 12 for instructions on faux mitered corners.)

15. Edge stitch ⅛" away from the inside of your trim. Use your magic H foot to guide the inner edge of the bias and move your needle to the left for a nice straight line. (See page 6 for advice on using the Super H foot.) At each corner, leave your needle down in the pillow trim; lift your presser foot and pivot the pillow cover. Line up the inner edge of the trim again and continue until all four of your corners are complete.

16. To finish the trim, overlap the trim ¾" and pin it into place. Before stitching, check your pillow back to make sure it is lined up and even. Edge stitch into place and don't forget to backstitch. (See page 13 for information on finishing trim.)

17. Insert a 16" pillow form into your brand new pillow and enjoy!

3

For You

Makeup Bag

Makeup Bag

Finished Dimensions: 7" (L) × 6" (H) × 2½" (D)

Oilcloth and makeup bags were made for each other. Any woman who ever had her powder compact open inside her makeup bag and then turn to dust would probably agree. Oilcloth is waterproof and so easy to clean it's just perfect for this project; any mess wipes clean easily. This pattern is modeled after a beloved makeup bag that was ruined on my last flight. I know my new oilcloth makeup bag will wash right up even if the baggage handlers crush another jar of foundation.

> June Suggests: Even though oilcloth is durable, easy-to-clean, and waterproof, it can stain when met with a bright red lipstick, so use a dark-colored lining fabric. Better yet, use a crazy print and those stains won't stand a chance.

Materials

2 fat quarters of coordinating oilcloth (1 for the exterior, 1 for the lining). If purchasing off the roll, ask for ¼ yard of each.

11" zipper

Matching thread

Point turner

Note: The sample is shown with three oilcloth prints but the instructions are for two. Feel free to be creative and use one, two, or three oilcloths to make your special makeup case.

Mark It Up and Cut It Out

Draw the following on the back of the oilcloth pieces and cut out (see layout diagrams):

From the exterior material: Cut one 8" × 15" rectangle (for the outer main body) and two 3½" × 5½" rectangles (for the outer side panels).

From the lining material: Cut one 8" × 15" rectangle (for the inner main body), two 3½" × 5½" rectangles (for the inner side panels), and two 1" × 16" strips (for the trim and tabs).

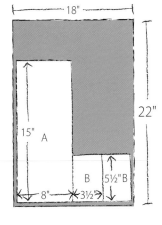

Exterior oilcloth

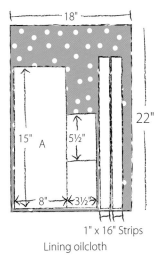

1" x 16" Strips

Lining oilcloth

Steps

1. With the right sides facing, pair one of the small exterior rectangles with one of the small lining rectangles. Align all of the edges. Use a ¼" seam allowance to stitch around the long side edges and the short bottom edge. The short top edge should be left open at this point. Repeat with the remaining small rectangles. Clip the bottom corners (see the illustration) and turn the pieces right side out. Use a point turner (or something similar, such as a chopstick or knitting needle) to make the corners sharp and then book press the pieces (see page 9 for information about book pressing).

2. Cut a 3½" piece from one of the 16" strips. Fold the strip in half lengthwise and crease press (see the tip on page 9). Fold the short ends under ¼" to the wrong side. With the exterior of one of the side panels face up, sandwich the folded trim over the top edge and arrange the folded short ends so they line up with the edges of the side panel (see the illustration). After you have both ends flush and nicely finished off, pin the trim in place along the stitch line and then edge stitch the trim into place about ⅛" from the edge. (For great tips on edge stitching trim into place, see page 9.)

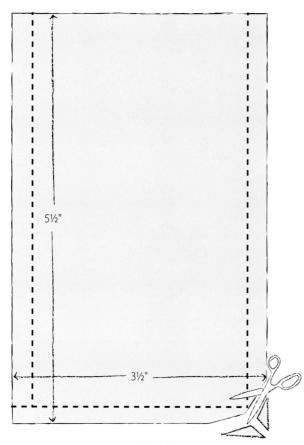

Step 1

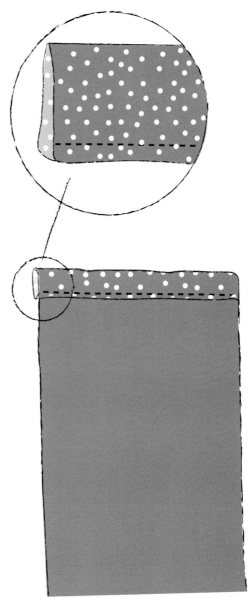

Step 2

3. Use the second 16" strip to make a snazzy little strap for your makeup bag. Apply it to the second side panel as described in Step 2, turning under and aligning the ends and edge stitching it into place, but this time continue sewing the remainder of the trim together by edge stitching the folded trim that extends beyond the side panel.

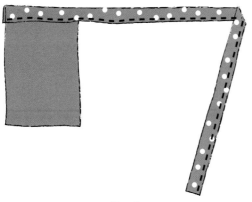

Step 3

4. To create the main body of the makeup bag, place the large rectangles together, right sides facing and align all of the edges. Stitch together, ¼" from the two long edges (the short edges should be left open at this point). Be sure to backstitch when you start and stop each stitch line. Carefully and slowly turn the piece right side out. With your fingers flatten your seams until they are straight and even. Baste the two open edges closed using a ⅛" seam allowance. Then book press the piece as you did with the side panels in Step 1.

5. Fold each of the side panels in half lengthwise, and place pins at the position of the folds to mark the centers. (Remember: Pins can leave holes so just slide the pins into the seams near the bottom edge.)

6. Fold the main body in half widthwise, and mark the center with pins on both long edges of the piece. Place a pin along the long side of the main piece 1" down from the top edge.

7. With the lining sides facing together, match the center of one side panel with the center of the left side of the main body and pin ⅛" away from the edge. Repeat with the second side panel and the right side of the main body. (See the illustration.)

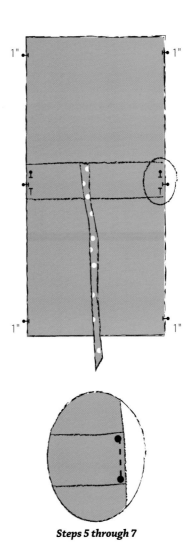

Steps 5 through 7

8. Edge stitch the side panels using a ⅛" seam allowance, leaving ⅛" free on both ends of each side panel. You have now created the bottom of your makeup bag.

9. Bring the corner of the side panel that has the overhanging strap up to meet the adjacent 1" pin mark on the main body. Align the edges in between. Tuck ½" of the strap end in between the body and side panel lining layers. Pin together and then stitch ⅛" from the aligned edges. The main body will kind of round out near the bottom corners of each side piece. Finger press them and pin the corners. Stitch ⅛" from the aligned edges.

10. Repeat the alignment and stitching process for the other three panel/main body edges.

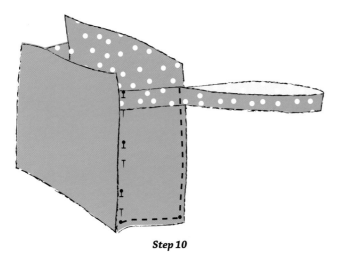

Step 10

11. You need to shorten your zipper, so close the zipper and measure 9½" away from the open (pinked) end of the zipper and make a mark with a pencil. Create a bar tack by making 8 to 10 whip stitches (with a double thread) tightly across the coil or teeth at the mark. Cut the zipper ½" below the bar tack so that you have a 10" zipper.

12. ½" above the metal stops, whip-stitch the open end of the zipper closed as well. It's easier to do this with the zipper completely closed.

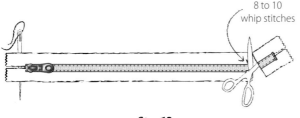

8 to 10 whip stitches

Step 12

13. Now your zipper is ready for some fun oilcloth tabs. Cut two 1" × 3¼" pieces from the trim strip and make two loops by bringing the short ends together (right sides facing) and stitching using a ¼" seam allowance. Flip the loop so that the right side of the oilcloth is facing out.

14. Edge stitch ⅛" from the two short ends and one long end (leaving one long end unsewn) to create a small pocket. Slide the small oilcloth tabs onto the ends of the zipper and stitch the tab closed ⅛" from the remaining long end. (See the illustration.)

Step 14

15. Use a pin or chalk to mark the center of your 10" zipper. Also mark the center of the top edge of your bag by making a tiny clip in the very center of the front and back of the main body.

16. Match the center of the zipper to the center of the front of the main body with the working side of the zipper facing the right side of the exterior material, and pin the zipper in place.

17. Using a ⅛" seam allowance, stitch the zipper to the bag and then fold the seam allowance up and under. Your zipper is now face up. Finger press (see the tip on finger pressing on page 9) a crease into the fold and then edge stitch, making sure to backstitch at the beginning and end of the stitching.

18. Turn your makeup bag inside out and repeat Steps 16 and 17 along the back side of the makeup bag.

19. Flip the bag right side out, and you have a sweet makeup bag.

Wallet

Wallet

Finished Dimensions: 7¹/₂" by 4" (closed)

Oilcloth makes for a fun wallet. Every time you pay for something you'll get lots of compliments. This snappy little wallet secures your money, receipts, money card, and ID, and it's slim enough to fit into even the smallest of purses.

> June Suggests: This is a great project for using up your scraps, so go crazy and make each pocket a different print. Use a bright print and you'll never lose your wallet in your handbag again.

Materials

¹/₄ yard of 47"/48" oilcloth

2 pearl snaps

Coordinating thread

Point turner

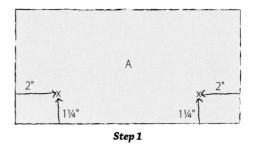

Step 1

Mark It Up and Cut It Out

1. Draw one 3" × 8½" rectangle on the back of the oilcloth for the small pocket and cut it out. Use a pencil to label this Piece A by writing the letter A in the seam allowance near the bottom of the pocket. Draw two X's on the wrong side of the oilcloth 2" in from each side edge and 1¼" up from the bottom on each side of Piece A. (See the illustration.)

2. Draw one 3½" × 8½" rectangle on the back of the oilcloth for the middle pocket and cut it out. Use a pencil to label this Piece B by writing the letter B in the seam allowance near the bottom of the pocket. With your pencil draw a line down the center of the Pocket B to split it horizontally.

3. Draw two 4" × 8½" rectangles on the back of the oilcloth for the largest pocket and cut them out. Mark these large pockets with the letter C.

4. Draw an 8½" × 16" rectangle on the back of the oilcloth for the exterior of your wallet and cut it out. Mark this as Piece D.

Steps

1. Follow the manufacturer's directions to apply the bottom half of the two snaps onto Piece A. The working side of the snap should be on the right side of the fabric.

2. On Pieces A and B, turn the top edge over ½" to the wrong side and pin at the sides (to avoid pin holes). Topstitch in place using a ⅜" seam allowance. (See the illustration.)

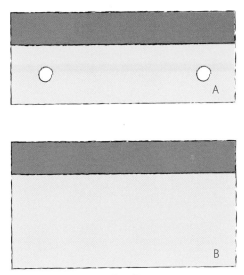

Step 2

3. Place Piece A on top of Piece B so that both are facing right side up. Align the bottom edges and pin the two pieces together along the side seam allowances. Baste the pieces together along the sides and bottom using a ⅛" seam allowance.

4. Turn the two layers face down, and from the wrong side of Piece B stitch along the center line you drew when you cut out the piece. Make sure to backstitch at the top of Piece A. This stitch line creates two smaller pockets in Piece A. (See the illustration.)

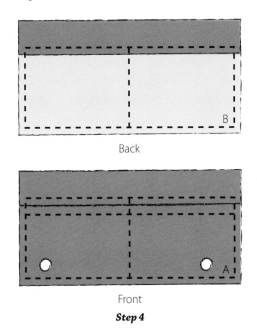

Back

Front

Step 4

5. Place the two C pieces together with the right sides facing and sew them along one of the long sides, ¼" from the aligned edges. Unfold the piece you just created so that it is a single layer with a seam in the middle.

6. With the right sides facing up, place Pieces A and B on Piece C, aligning the bottoms of all the pockets. Pin and then baste them together along the side and bottom using a ⅛" seam allowance. (See the illustration.)

7. Fold over the upper layer of Pocket C so that the right side is facing the front of the pockets. Pin and sew the side seams shut, ¼" from the edges.

8. Grade the seam allowance (see page 10 for more information on grading seams) and clip the corners to reduce bulk. (See the illustration.)

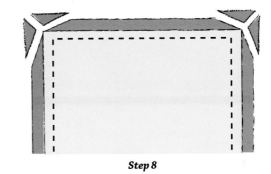

Step 8

9. Turn the completed pocket section so the right side is facing out. Carefully use a point turner to make sure you have crisp corners along the top edge. Topstitch the top long edge of Piece C using a ⅜" seam allowance for a nice professional look.

10. Fold Piece D (the wallet exterior) in half widthwise with the right sides together so you have an 8" × 8½" piece. Pin along the two 8" sides and stitch, making sure to backstitch at the beginning and the end of both seams. Grade the seam allowance and clip the corners as you've done in the previous step.

11. Turn the wallet exterior right side out and use a point turner on your corners as you did in Step 9. Book press until the exterior is flat and crisp. (See page 9 for information about book pressing.)

12. Along the 7½" finished edge of Piece D, apply the second half of the two snaps through both layers of the wallet. To make sure the two halves of the snap are aligned, mark an X 1¾" in from each side edge and ¾" up from the top on each corner. This top edge is your wallet's flap. Apply the snaps at the two X marks according to manufacturer's directions. (See the illustration.) The working side of the snap should be on the side that faces the inside of the wallet.

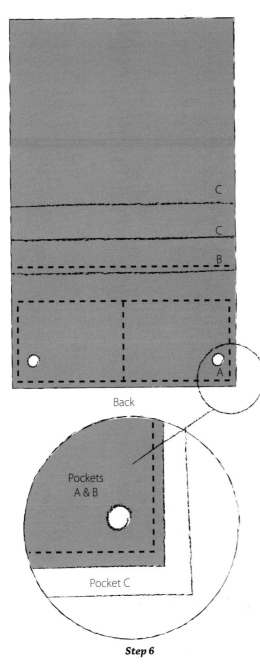

Back

Pockets
A & B

Pocket C

Step 6

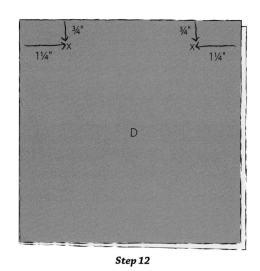

Step 12

13. Line up the unfinished edge of the pocket section and the unfinished edge of the main wallet piece. The front side of the pocket section should be facing the side that will end up on the exterior of the wallet. Pin and sew them together, ¼" from the aligned edges. Next grade and clip the seam allowance. (See the illustration.)

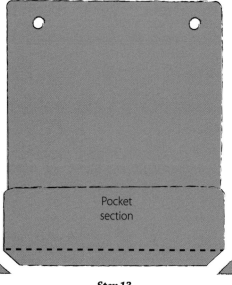

Pocket section

Step 13

14. Flip the pocket section around to the other side of the wallet's interior. This encloses the seam allowance created in Step 12 and creates another pocket. Use a clothespin to secure the pockets to the wallet sides and use your hands to crease press the wallet to help create a crease along this rather thick seam. (See pages 7 and 9 for advice on pinning and crease pressing.)

15. Edge stitch (see page 9 for details on edge stitching) the sides and the top edge of the wallet. Doing so attaches the sides of the pockets to the wallet and finishes the wallet. Make sure to backstitch at the top of the pocket section. (See the illustration.)

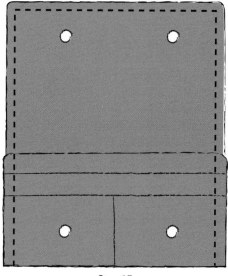

Step 15

16. Now just fill up your new wallet and go shopping!

Farmers Market Tote

Farmers Market Tote

Finished Dimensions: 11" inches wide at bottom × 8" (D) × 13" (L)

Nothing says spring and summer more than heading out to the farmers market every Saturday morning. This tote keeps all your fresh produce and flowers neat and orderly! I love the four exterior pockets for my herbs and flowers and the interior pocket is a safe place to stash my money. But the best thing about using oilcloth for a market tote is how well it cleans up. If your tomatoes make a mess you're covered; just wipe the tote down with a wet cloth, and you're ready to go.

June Suggests: Play with this pattern! Simplify it by leaving off the outer pockets or leaving it unlined. Also, you can change the look by changing the fabric prints. I used four prints, but you can totally change the look by using only one or two prints. Go sophisticated with the Mexican lace print, go perky with dots, or go country cute with gingham. Another alternative is to use laminated cotton for this fun bag. Just flat-line the outer pockets and lining with a firm interfacing to make the tote more stable.

Materials

1 yard of 47"/48" oilcloth for main tote

1 yard of 47"/48" oilcloth for lining and exterior pocket trim

½ yard of 47"/48" oilcloth for exterior side pockets

1 fat quarter 47"/48" oilcloth for exterior center pocket and interior pocket trim

1 spool coordinating thread for each oilcloth print

52" of 1" webbing for strap

Clear ruler

Craft paper or poster board

Pencil

Lighter

Binder clips (optional)

Seam gauge

Mark It Up and Cut It Out

Making a pattern is very easy and extraordinarily satisfying. With a pencil, a wide, clear ruler, and some paper, you can use the following steps to make one in no time.

1. To create Piece A, use a clear, wide ruler or square to trace a 19" × 20" rectangle onto a piece of paper or poster board. Then use your ruler to mark two 4" squares in two of the corners along one of the 20" sides of the rectangle. This portion between the squares will become the bottom of the tote. Mark the pattern with the letter A. Cut out the large rectangle and then cut out the two 4" squares in each of the bottom corners. Set aside Piece A.

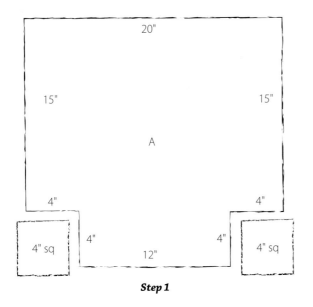

Step 1

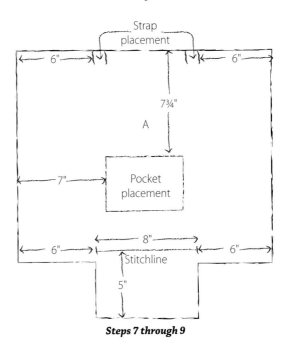

5. Piece E is a 2" × 42" strip that is used to trim the outer pockets. You can either make a pattern and trace, or directly mark cutting lines on the wrong side of the material.

6. Piece F is a 1" × 7" strip. Draw it on your paper or poster board, cut it out, and mark it F. This will be the trim for your outer pocket. You can either make a pattern and trace, or directly mark cutting lines on the wrong side of the material.

7. You need to mark several items on Piece A to guide you as you sew. Start with marking the strap placement by making a few small pencil lines along the top of the tote pattern. The first one is 6" from the left-hand corner along the top 20" of the tote; the second one is 1" away from the first one, toward the center. Repeat the process on the other side. (See the illustration.)

8. Mark pattern A for the interior pocket placement. Take Piece D and use it to trace your pocket guide on the tote pattern by centering Piece D on Piece A. The top edge of the pocket is 7¾" from the tote's top edge, and the side of the pocket is 7" away from the tote's side. Cut this small rectangle out of the center of Piece A. (See the illustration.)

9. Add a stitch line to Piece A by measuring up 5" from the bottom edge of Piece A and drawing an 8" line that is centered. The line starts 6" from the two sides of the pattern. (See the illustration.)

2. Piece B, the center pocket for the exterior of the tote, is a simple 9" × 14" rectangle. Measure the rectangle onto your paper or poster board, mark it as B, and then cut it out.

3. For the side exterior pockets, Pattern Piece C, draw a 6½" × 14" rectangle on your paper or poster board. Use your clear ruler to measure one 4" square in the corner to create the bottom of the pattern. Cut out your pattern as you did in Step 1. (Don't forget to create the 4" cut out.) Mark the pattern with the letter C.

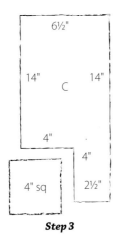

Step 3

4. For Piece D, the small interior pocket, measure and cut out a 4½" × 7" rectangle and mark it with a D.

Steps 7 through 9

10. Using the following information and the pattern layout illustration, trace the pattern pieces onto your oilcloth and then cut them out.

Print for exterior of tote	Print for interior of tote and exterior trim	Print for exterior side pockets and small interior pocket	Print for exterior center pockets and interior pocket trim
Cut 2 Piece A	Cut 2 Piece A	Cut 4 Piece C (2 pairs of mirror image pieces)	Cut 2 Piece B
	Cut 1 Piece E	Cut 1 Piece D	Cut 1 Piece F

11. Mark your interior pocket placement on the back side of one of the lining pieces (that you cut using Piece A).

12. On the wrong sides of both of the exterior tote pieces, use Pattern Piece A to transfer the strap placement and the center pocket stitch line.

13. Cut the webbing into two 26" lengths to be used as the tote's straps. To keep the straps from fraying you need to seal them by carefully burning the cut ends of the webbing straps with the flame of a lighter.

This won't take long; you don't want the webbing to shrink and curl. You just want the ends to become shiny and slightly melted so that the webbing doesn't fray out.

Note: Please be cautious when melting the nylon. Keep it away from your skin and only do this in a well-ventilated area.

Steps

1. Take one of your outer pocket pieces (Piece B) and arrange it with two of the side pocket pieces (Piece C) so that the two long sides of the side pocket pieces are aligned with the long edges of the outer pocket with the right sides together. (See the illustration.) Pin them and then stitch with a ½" seam allowance. Repeat with the second set of pocket pieces.

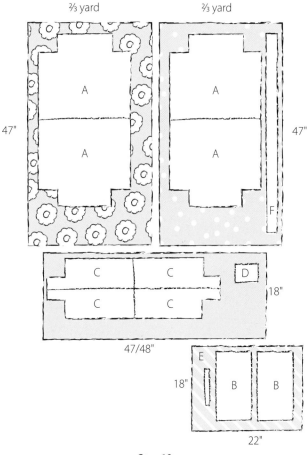

Step 10

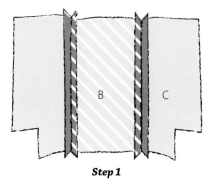

Step 1

2. Arrange the two pieces you created in Step 1 so they're aligned along the long edge of the side pockets, pin them, and sew them together at the side seams with a ½" seam allowance, leaving the other side open for now. Now you have one long pocket section. (See the illustration.)

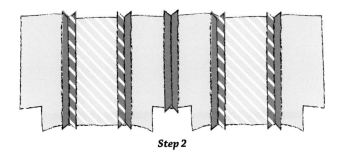

Step 2

3. Book press the center pocket seams toward the center and book press the side seam to the left while you prep the pocket trim. (See page 9 for information on book pressing.)

4. Fold the outer pocket trim (Piece E) in half the long way and crease press it (see page 9 for information on crease pressing).

5. Sandwich the top edge of the joined pocket pieces within the folded trim (Piece E). The trim should be flush on the starting end and should have an extra 2" hanging off the other end. Pin the trim into place and then edge stitch, stopping 2" from the edge of the pocket so that the last 4" of trim are unstitched and open. (See the illustration.)

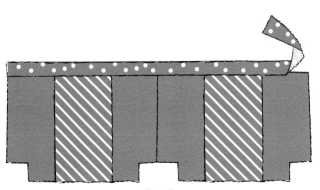

Step 5

6. Put the two main tote exterior pieces (Piece A) right sides together, pin, and stitch one of the sides with a ½" seam allowance. Finger press the side seam to the right. (See page 9 for information on finger pressing.)

7. Center your pocket section on your pieced tote exterior so that both are right sides up—align the bottom edges of the two pieces. Pin along the bottom of tote. Then pin down the center pocket as shown in the illustration. (Take my word for it: Even if you're a seasoned seamstress like me you'll want to pin this as shown in the illustration!)

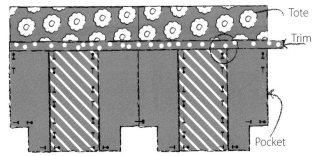

Step 7

8. Topstitch along the side edges of each center pocket, about ⅛" from the seams. Be sure to backstitch at the top of each pocket to protect from normal wear and tear. (See the illustration.)

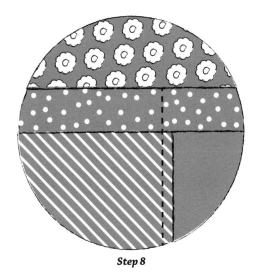

Step 8

9. Place the tote upside down on your work surface and pin just below your center pocket stitch line. Make sure that your thread and bobbin match the outer center pocket oilcloth. Sew along the stitch line you drew to close off the bottom of your center pocket between the vertical stitch lines. (See the illustration.)

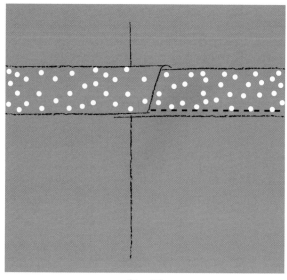

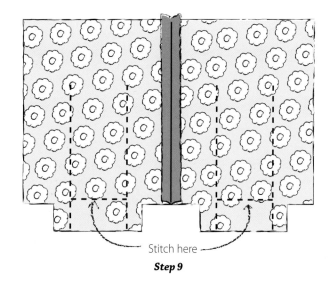

Stitch here

Step 9

10. Close the other set of side seams starting with the pocket layer. With the trim moved out of your way, pin the seam with the right sides together and sew the seam, ½" from the aligned edges. Finger press the seam to the left.

11. Place your tote flat on your work surface so that the right side of the newly sewn side seam is facing you. Cut the loose end of the trim down so that there is 1" left to overlap the trim on the finished side. Then sandwich this trim over the side seam on to the completed side pocket. Pin the trim into place, being careful to match up the trim so it is one nice straight line and edge stitch the trim to the pocket. (See the illustration.)

Step 11

12. Pin and sew up the other side seam on the main body layer of the tote.

13. Match your edges on the bottom of the tote and pin all four layers together. Stitch the bottom of the tote shut ½" from the aligned bottom edges and then finger press the seam to one side.

14. Pinch the corners together by matching your side seam to the bottom seam and flattening the bag to create a straight edge. Pin and sew. (See the illustration.)

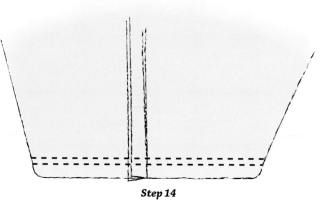

Step 14

15. Attach the webbing straps by pinning the ends in place against the right side of the bag and zigzag-stitching with a ¼" seam allowance. Repeat the zigzag stitch three times for added strength.

Step 15

Note: If you aren't going to line your tote, skip to Step 23.

16. Trim the top of the inner pocket (Piece D) with the 1" oilcloth strip (Piece F). Crease fold the trim lengthwise and then sandwich the trim around the top of the inner pocket. The ends of the trim should be flush with the short ends of the pocket piece.

17. Edge stitch the trim.

18. Pin the inner pocket into place on one of your tote lining pieces. Edge stitch your inner pocket into place, making sure to backstitch at the tops of the pocket as this is a place of normal wear and tear.

19. Place your two tote lining pieces together and sew the side seams and bottom seam.

20. Sew the corners of the lining together by matching up your side seam to the bottom seam and flattening the bag to create a straight edge. Pin and sew. See Step 14 and its illustration for more information.

21. Slide your constructed lining down into the tote exterior. Make sure you get each corner of the lining neatly in place; the seams at the corner will want to fold toward the top of the tote. You might need to slide your hand down between the lining and tote to keep the corners tidy. Be patient; this is a fussy job.

22. When the lining is neatly in place, pin the lining and the exterior together at the side seams starting about 3" below the top of the tote. Remember to pin in the seam to avoid pin marks.

23. Using a seam gauge, fold the top of the tote exterior over 1" to the wrong side. (This is a great place to use binder clips as an alternative to pinning.) Then fold the lining toward the tote exterior so it is even with the top of tote. As you pin the lining and the tote together, place your hand inside the tote's lining to make sure that the lining is smooth. Make sure the straps are pulled up and outside of the tote.

Note: If you don't have a free arm sewing machine, just pin and sew from the lining side of the tote.

24. Finish the tote top by stitching two rows of topstitching. Stitch the first row ¼" from the folded edges and the second row ¾" from the folded edges. If your machine lets you, set your needle to stop with your needle down in the fabric to help you stitch a straight line as you move around the top of the tote. Go slow and be patient; this topstitching is tedious, but you're in the home stretch! You might need to stitch a few inches and then adjust the tote before going forward.

25. You're all done. Now it's time to go to the farmers market and fill up your fancy new tote!

Messenger Bag

Messenger Bag

Finished Dimensions: 14" wide at bottom × 6" (D) × 11" (L)

Messenger bags are the perfect all-purpose bags! I've used one as a school bag, a casual briefcase, a fun diaper bag, and as a weekend suitcase. Whatever your intended purpose, this project is loaded with a ton of pockets to keep you organized.

> **June Suggests:** This is another great project to use up all your scraps. Use a different print for each piece for a crazy patchwork messenger bag. I've used faux bois print to get the guys interested, but I've added a sophisticated lace oilcloth to the interior pockets to keep it interesting for us gals. If you are going to make one for your man, you can choose a gingham or a solid for the pockets.

Materials

1 yard of 47"/48" oilcloth for bag exterior and pocket linings

²/₃ yard of 47"/48" oilcloth for bag interior

¹/₂ yard of 47"/48" oilcloth for contrasting pockets and pocket linings

1¹/₄ yard of heavyweight interfacing

2 packages of ¹/₂"-wide cotton double-fold bias tape

1¹/₂ yard of webbing

Clear wide ruler or square

Dry erase marker

1 magnetic snap

1 1" strap adjuster

Coordinating thread

Mark It Up and Cut It Out

1. There are several pattern pieces for the messenger bag, but they are very simple shapes. Use a clear, wide ruler or square to measure your patterns onto poster board. Make sure to label each of your patterns with the appropriate letter.

Measure and cut out the following pattern pieces:

Pattern A	12" × 15" for front and back panels
Pattern B	6" × 12" for side panels
Pattern C	13" × 14" for flap (see Step 3 for more information)
Pattern D	6" × 8" × 8" for interior drink pocket (see Step 4 for more information)
Pattern E	6" × 8" for large exterior side pocket
Pattern F	6" × 6" for small exterior side pocket
Pattern G	9" × 15" for large interior and exterior pockets
Pattern H	6" × 15" for segmented interior pocket
Pattern I	6" × 15" for bottom

Note: All pattern pieces include a ¹/₂" seam allowance.

2. Place an X for the snap on to Pattern A that is 5" down from one of the long edges of the pattern and centered widthwise (7½" from the short side).

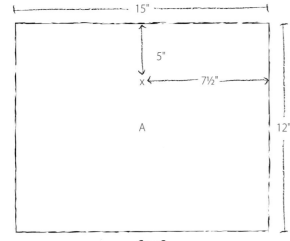

Step 2

3. To create Pattern C, measure the 13" × 14" rectangle and trace a 3" circle into the lower corners. Cut the rounded corners by following the curve. Mark a + for the snap, 2" up from the bottom edge in the center. (See the illustration.)

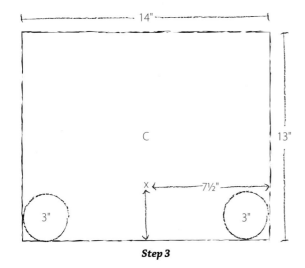

Step 3

4. For Pattern D, draw an 8" square and use a clear ruler to create a pattern that tapers from 8" at the top to 6" at the bottom. Cut away the angles. (See the illustration.)

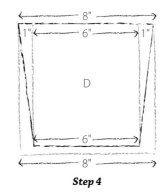

Step 4

5. On Pattern I, use a ruler to draw a dot in the top left-hand corner. The dot should be ½" away from the short edge and ½" away from the long side. Repeat on the other four corners.

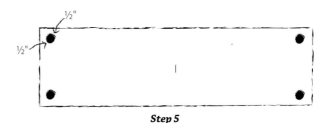

Step 5

6. Using the following information, cut the appropriate number of pieces from the fabrics and interfacing as described. Write the letter of each piece in pencil on the wrong side of the fabric. Transfer the dots on Pattern I onto the wrong sides of all Pieces I.

Pattern piece	Print #1 for exterior of bag and pocket linings	Print #2 for interior of bag	Print #3 for contrasting pockets and pocket linings	Interfacing
A	Cut 2	Cut 2		Cut 2
B	Cut 2	Cut 2		Cut 2
C	Cut 1	Cut 1		Cut 1
D	Cut 1		Cut 1	
E	Cut 1		Cut 1	
F	Cut 1		Cut 1	
G	Cut 2		Cut 2	
H	Cut 1		Cut 1	
I	Cut 1		Cut 1	

Steps

1. Flat-line the interfacing to the coordinating exterior Pieces A, B, and C by stitching all four sides of the pieces together with a ⅛" seam allowance. (See page 10 for information about flat-lining.)

2. Prepare all pockets by matching each pocket with its lining piece. The pieces should be paired with the wrong sides together. Pin the pieces at the seam sides or along the bottom. Sandwich the top of each pocket inside the ½" bias tape and edge stitch the trim into place. I like to chain stitch them (as shown in the illustration) into the bias to save time. (See page 9 for more information about edge stitching.)

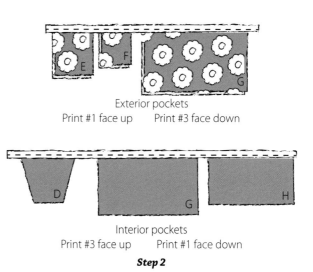

Exterior pockets
Print #1 face up   Print #3 face down

Interior pockets
Print #3 face up   Print #1 face down
Step 2

3. Cut each pocket loose from the bias strip and trim the ends flush with the side edges. Start making your pocket units by laying Pocket H on top of Pocket G so that both face right side up. Align the pieces along the bottom edge and pin the two pockets together along the side seam allowances. Baste the pockets together along the sides and bottom using a ¼" seam allowance.

4. With a dry erase marker, draw a line down the center of Pocket H. (Test your marker on a scrap first and make sure it wipes clean.) Mark a second and third line to the left, 1½" apart. Sewing with print #3 facing up, stitch Pocket H to Pocket G along the lines, which creates the bag's pen and pencil slots. (See the illustration.)

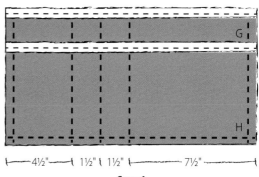

├──4½"──┤ 1½" ┤ 1½" ├────7½"────┤
Step 4

5. Layer the pocket unit made in Step 4 on top of a lining Piece A. With all sides facing right side up, align the side and bottom edges, pin, and baste together.

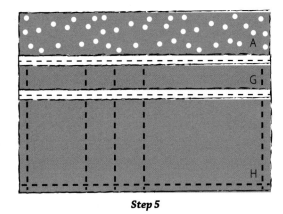

Step 5

6. To make the angled drink pocket, pin Pocket D to one of your lining side panels (Piece B) along the bottom. Bring the side of Pocket D flush with the side of lining Piece B and pin into place. Repeat with the other side. Pocket D now bows out to create a handy catch-all pocket for drinks or your cell phone. (See the illustration.)

Step 6

7. Layer Pocket F onto Pocket E with both facing right side up. Remember: These pockets go on the outside of the messenger bag so place print #1 face up. Baste the pockets together with a ¼" seam allowance at the sides and bottom so that the two become one unit. Then baste them onto an exterior side Piece B. (See the illustration.)

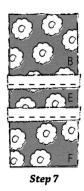

Step 7

8. To make the flap for the bag, follow the manufacturer's directions to add one half of the snap to the place you marked with the + on lining Piece C. Then layer the lining Piece C with exterior Piece C, pin, and trim the side and bottom edges with the ½" cotton bias tape as you did with the pockets.

9. Place the other half of the snap on to one of the Piece A. This will become the bag's front exterior panel; the snap will be near the top edge of the bag.

10. Take your 1" webbing and cut it into two pieces; the first piece should be 36" long and the second 18" long. Finish off the ends of both straps by carefully melting the ends with the lighter. This won't take long; you don't want the webbing to shrink and curl. You just want the ends to become shiny and slightly melted so that the webbing doesn't fray out. Make the strap by looping one end of the 36" piece of webbing through the strap adjuster; you should have a 2" tail. Pin and sew the tail to the strap with a double line of stitching to secure the strap adjuster within the webbing loop. Slide the 18" piece of webbing into the adjuster according to the manufacturer's instructions. After you add this to your messenger bag you'll be able to adjust the shorter strap for your comfort.

Note: Please be cautious when melting the nylon. Keep it away from your skin and do this in a well-ventilated area.

11. Now that you have your pieces prepped it's time to put them together. Start with the exterior pieces. Pin Piece A with the snap to the Piece B with the pockets, making sure that the snap is at the top of Piece A and the pockets are at the bottom. Sew them together leaving the bottom ½" of the seam open. Now pin the second Piece A to the other side of Piece B and stitch, again leaving the bottom ½" open. Attach the second Piece B to the second Piece A. Lastly, close up the last seam by sewing the second Piece B to the original Piece A. You have a bag without a bottom.

12. Pin the exterior bottom (Piece I) to one Piece A with the right sides together. Sew from dot to dot (see the illustration) letting the ½" left open on each of the bag's side seams splay open. Make sure that you get all the extra fabric away from the seam by pinching and pulling it out of harm's way. Now you're ready to sew the first seam. Repeat with the other three sides.

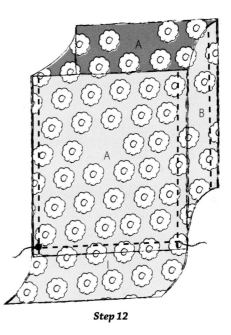

Step 12

13. Repeat Steps 11 and 12 with the lining pieces.

14. Trim the bottom of the bag's exterior to ¼" and clip the corners at an angle so there is less bulk in the corners. Flip it inside out. Turning the exterior can be very tricky; just go slowly and be patient, folding down a bit at a time. A little heat can soften the oilcloth and make turning easier. A few minutes out in the sun can help soften the oilcloth.

15. Pin the bag's flap (Piece C) onto the back Piece A with the exterior sides together and baste in place using a ¼" seam allowance. The flap will fit from seam to seam across the back.

16. Slide the lining into the messenger bag. Because you can't iron your oilcloth seams open, crease press the exterior seams in the opposite direction as the lining seams to reduce bulk at the side seams. Pin around the top and baste the two together.

17. Trim out the top edge of the bag with the bias. (See page 11 for information on finishing bias.)

19. Attach the straps by centering each strap 3" down from the top edge and pinning it into place. Sew a 1" box and then stitch an X within the box. Stitch through every layer for added strength. (See the illustration.)

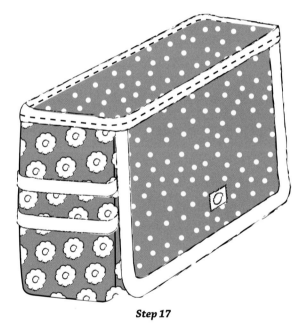

Step 17

18. Flip the bias tape concealed edge of the flap down against the bag lining and topstitch it into place.

Step 19

20. Now it's time to move your loot into the messenger bag and hit the road.

Sandwich Wrapper

Sandwich Wrapper

Finished Dimensions: 15" square

Laminated cotton is a great choice for this handy sandwich wrapper because it's water-resistant and it cleans up wonderfully. Combine that with being BPA and PVC-free and you have a great way for the entire family to save on all those pesky plastic bags. You'll always have a clean place to eat lunch when your open wrapper turns into a placemat. Just wipe with a damp sponge and hang to dry and you're ready for a meal on-the-go.

> **June Suggests:** Go crazy and mix and match your laminated cotton prints; use a coordinating print for the lining and another for the exterior. Have a really snazzy lunch set up and make yourself the matching snack bag and lunch bag found on page 90 and page 95.

Materials

Note: Oilcloth contains phthalates and is not to be used for projects intended for children under the age of 12 or for projects that come in direct contact with food, so this project uses laminated cotton. Please do not substitute oilcloth for this project.

1/2 yard of 54"/56" laminated cotton

Small package of double-sided iron-on adhesive interfacing

One package of contrasting 1/4" double-fold bias tape

1 yard of 1/4" grosgrain ribbon

Small bottle of liquid fabric sealant

Coordinating thread

Clear wide ruler or square

Rotary cutter (optional)

Cutting mat (optional)

Press cloth/clean white tea towel

Mark It Up and Cut It Out

1. Using a ruler and pencil trace two 15" squares on the wrong side of your laminated cotton. Use a clear, wide ruler or pattern square to make sure that your corners are all at 90° angles and then cut out your laminated cotton squares.

2. Repeat the previous step to cut out a single 15" square of iron-on adhesive interfacing.

Steps

1. Lay one of your laminated cotton squares onto your ironing board with the wrong side up. Layer the iron-on adhesive interfacing square on top of the laminated cotton so that the paper side is up; that way the glue side of the interfacing is facing the wrong side of the first laminated cotton square. Carefully match the two squares so there is no interfacing hanging off the edge of the wrapper.

2. Iron the adhesive interfacing onto the laminated cotton according to the manufacturer's instructions. Be patient and use a low temperature iron. The interfacing takes a few minutes to properly adhere. Pay close attention to the corners and let the layers cool before removing the paper.

3. Start peeling the paper off the interfacing at one of the corners and remove it completely. If you a see a spot where the glue isn't attached to the laminated cotton, just lay the paper back down and re-iron that spot. Be sure to keep the layer of glue away from your iron. (See the illustration.)

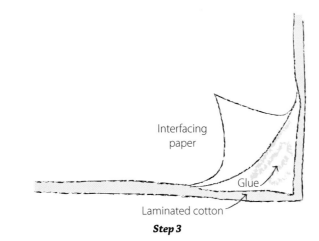

Step 3

4. Now that the glue is adhered and the paper is removed, lay the wrong side of the second laminated cotton square onto the newly exposed glue side of the interfacing. Again, carefully match the corners and edges of the layers. Gently place a clean press cloth onto the wrapper and iron as you did in Step 2.

5. To make the ties, take your 36" piece of grosgrain ribbon and fold it so that one side is 10" long and the other side is 26". (See the illustration.) Use a few drops of the liquid fabric sealant to keep the ends of the ribbon from unraveling. After the ends of the ribbon are dry, pin the ribbon onto one of the corners.

Step 5

6. Trim your wrapper by sandwiching the ¼" bias tape around the edge of your wrapper. Start trimming your sandwich wrapper about 6" away from the corner that has the ribbon ties pinned into place. Edge stitch the trim into place until you reach a corner. (See page 9 for information about edge stitching.)

7. At the corner, create a faux mitered corner, enclosing the ribbon ties within the stitches as shown in the illustration. (See page 12 for information on creating a faux mitered corner.)

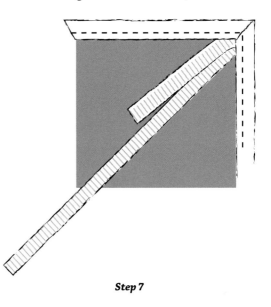

Step 7

8. After you have made your fourth mitered corner, cut off any extra bias by lining up the bias against the untrimmed section and adding an extra 1½". Sandwich the remainder of the bias in place, overlapping the trim 1" and tucking in ½" of bias at the end. Pin into place and sew. (For more information on finishing off cotton bias tape, see page 11.)

9. The only thing left to do now is to make a sandwich and wrap it up! To fold the wrapper around your sandwich, place your sandwich in the center of the mat with the ties of the wrapper on the top corner. Fold the side corners toward the center, fold up the bottom corner, and then fold down the top corner. Wrap the long side of the ribbon around to meet up with the shorter side and tie a pretty little bow. Bon appétit!

Snack Bag

Snack Bag

Finished Dimensions: $3\frac{1}{2}$" × 4" (6" when closed)

You're going to love this project. It'll save you tons of plastic baggies and, thanks to the box-like shape, it's easy to fill. The lining is loose so you can slip it out and keep it clean. Laminated cotton is so easy to care for; just wipe it clean and air dry.

> **June Suggests:** Double the size of this bag and you have a great wet bag for all of life's messes. When you make your pattern, start with a 10" × 12" rectangle and then follow the pattern instructions as stated.

Materials

Note: Oilcloth contains phthalates and is not to be used for projects intended for children under the age of 12 or for projects that come in direct contact with food, so this project uses laminated cotton. Please do not substitute oilcloth for this project.

$\frac{1}{4}$ yard of 54"/55" laminated cotton for the exterior

$\frac{1}{4}$ yard of 54"/55" laminated cotton for the interior

$6\frac{3}{4}$" hook and loop tape

Clear, wide ruler or square

Poster board or paper for making patterns

Coordinating thread

Mark It Up and Cut It Out

Note: You could do this project without making a pattern, but you'll probably find you want to make a ton of snack bags, so it'll be easier if you start by making a pattern.

1. Using a clear, wide ruler or square, trace a 7" × 7" square onto a piece of poster board. Then use your ruler to mark two $1\frac{1}{4}$" squares along one of the 7" sides of the rectangle; this will become the bottom of the snack bag. (See the illustration.)

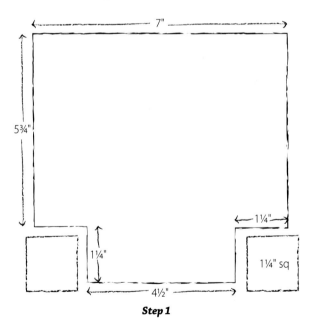

Step 1

2. Place together both Piece A exteriors with the right sides facing, pin, and stitch along the bottom and both sides, ½" from the aligned edges. Leave the notches open for now. Press the seams open, making sure to use a press cloth. (See page 9 for detailed information on ironing laminated cotton.) Trim the seam allowances to ¼".

3. Pinch the side seam and the bottom seam together. With the right sides facing, match the seams to make the corner of your bag and pin. Repeat on the other side and sew ½" from the aligned edges, being sure to backstitch at each side of the seam. (See the illustration.) Trim the seam allowances of your corners to ¼" and turn the piece right side out.

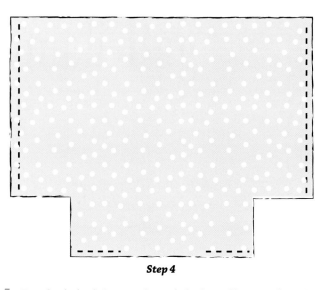

Step 4

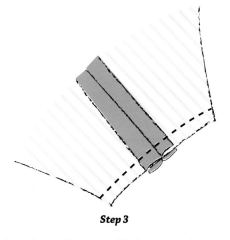

Step 3

4. Pin and stitch the side seams of the lining together as you did in Step 2 but along the bottom only sew 1½" inches along either side of the bottom edge. Make sure to backstitch. By doing so you are leaving the center of the bottom seam open. (See the illustration.)

5. To make the bag's flap, pin the angled sides and bottom edges of exterior Piece B and lining Piece B with the right sides facing. Sew with the interfacing face up so that the insulation doesn't get caught on the feed dogs of your machine. Grade the insulating interfacing and exterior fabric down to ¼" and then clip the corners of all three layers. Check out page 10 of the tip section to learn how to grade a seam.

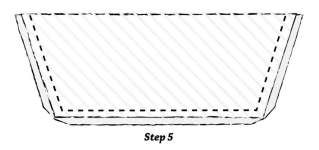

Step 5

6. Turn the flap inside out and press, making sure that the seams are as flat as possible. Using the manufacturer's directions, add one side of your magnetic snap into the lining of the flap. *Optional*: Topstitch the three finished sides of your flap with a ¼" seam allowance. (See the illustration.)

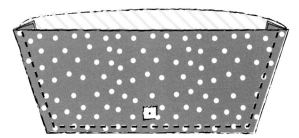

Step 6

7. Now that you have completed all your bag's pieces and parts, it's time to start putting them together. Turn the exterior piece so the right side is facing out. Start by adding the bag's 22" webbing strap to the right side by centering the 1" webbing over the two side seams. After you have made sure your strap is not twisted, baste it in place using a ¼" seam allowance.

8. Pin the flap (Piece B) onto the back side of your bag's exterior with exterior print facing exterior print. The edge of the flap matches up to the side seams of the bag, thus covering half of the webbing straps. Baste in place with a ¼" seam allowance.

Step 8

9. With the lining wrong side out, slide the exterior of the bag into the lining. Match the side seams, pin, and sew shut ½" from the aligned top edges. Work the bag out of the opening at the bottom of the lining; work it out slowly and carefully. Close up the opening of the lining by pinching the lining together and edge stitching it closed.

10. Slide the lining down into the bag, press, and topstitch using a ¼" seam allowance. Optional: Topstitch around the top circle of the bag, excluding the flap.

11. Now it's time to join the ladies that lunch, so fill 'er up!

For Kids

Baby Bib

Baby Bib

Finished Dimensions: Fits ages 6 months to 18 months

What I like best about using laminated cotton for baby items is that it's BPA and PVC free. I also like that it's waterproof, machine washable, and very pretty! The next time you're invited to a baby shower, make a few of these bibs, add a splat mat (the next project in this chapter), and you have the perfect gift. The mom-to-be will thank you again when the baby starts solids!

> June Suggests: Play with prints, go matchy-matchy, or use contrasting prints to make a full set of unique baby bibs. Please note that I don't recommend making reversible baby bibs with the laminated cotton because water collects between the layers, which makes the bibs take too long to dry out.

Materials

Note: Oilcloth contains phthalates and is not to be used for projects intended for children under the age of 12 or for projects that come in direct contact with food, so this project uses laminated cotton. Please do not substitute oilcloth for this project.

$1/2$ yard of 44"/45" or 54"/56" laminated cotton for baby bib

$1/8$ yard of 44"/45" or 54"/56" laminated cotton for pocket

One package of contrasting $1/2$" double-fold bias tape for the top edge of the pocket

One package of contrasting $1/4$" double-fold bias tape for the neckline and outer edging

2 pearl snaps

Coordinating thread

Mark It Up and Cut It Out

1. Photocopy Patterns A and B from pages 137–139. Make sure to enlarge them by the percentage printed on the pattern pieces.

2. Trace the patterns on your laminated cotton and cut out the pieces.

3. Mark the notches drawn on the patterns on your laminated cotton. Make your marks on the right side of the fabric, being sure to do it on the very edge of the bib and pocket.

4. Mark the placement of your snaps on the wrong side of your bib piece.

Steps

1. Cut an 11" piece of ½" bias tape and sandwich it along the top edge of the pocket. Pin it in place before edge stitching it. Trim off the extra bias at the edge of the pocket. (See the edge stitch tip on page 9.)

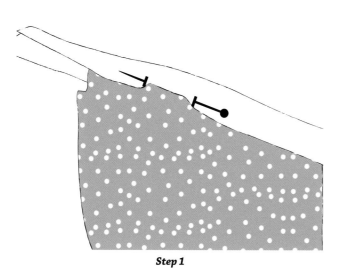

Step 1

2. With both the bib and pocket right side up, place the pocket right below the two side notches you marked on the bib and pin along the very edge of the fabric at each of the marks.

3. Match the center notch on the bib and pocket and pin into place along the edge of the fabric. Your pocket is a bit bigger than the bib so you need to ease the pocket around the bottom curve evenly and pin along the edge.

Note: By easing the pocket into place you're creating a pocket that stands away from the bib, which helps with catching crumbs.

4. Baste the pocket into place using a ⅛" seam allowance.

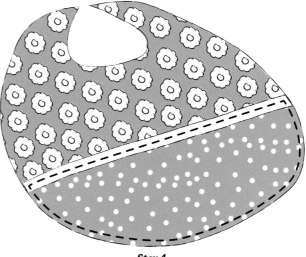

Step 4

5. Cut 41" of ¼" double-fold bias tape. Starting at Point A, sandwich the bias tape along the outer edge of the bib and pocket. Stop at Point B and cut any extra bias flush with the bib. Stitch into place, being sure to backstitch at each end.

6. Cut 18" of ¼" double-fold bias tape. Finish trimming the neckline of the bib by sandwiching the bias tape around the neck. Leave 1" at each end.

7. Fold the bias tabs to the wrong side of the bib and pin them in place, being careful not to pin into the laminated cotton.

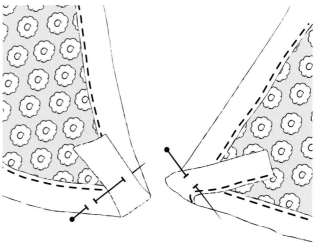

Step 7

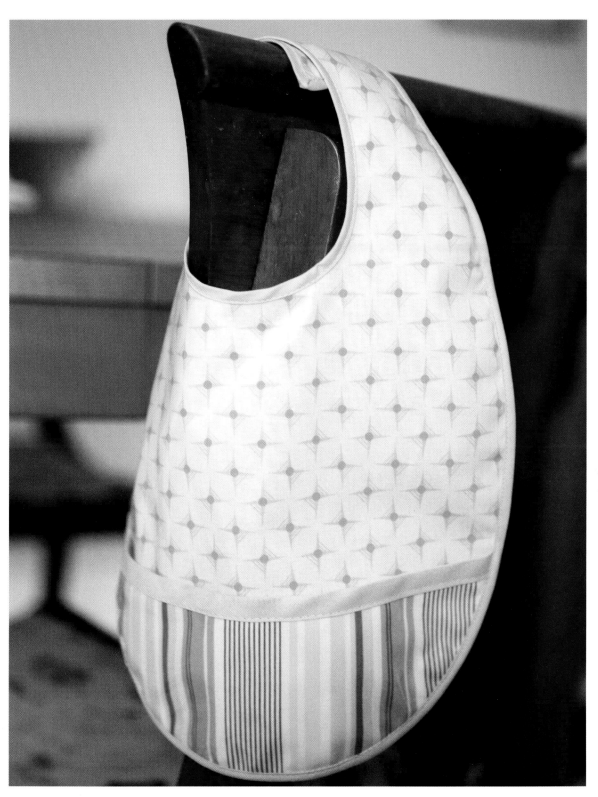

8. From the right side of the bib, stitch the bias tabs down, making sure to follow your previous stitch line.

Note: Repositioning your needle to the side can help line up your stitches nicely and enables you to use the presser foot as your guide. (See the "Super H" tip on page 9.)

9. Apply the snaps according to the manufacturer's instructions. Note that there are two snap points near the left hand corner. Apply two female snap halves at these points so that the working sides are on the right side of the material. On the other side, apply a single male snap so that the working side is on the wrong side of the material. Now you're ready for baby's next meal!

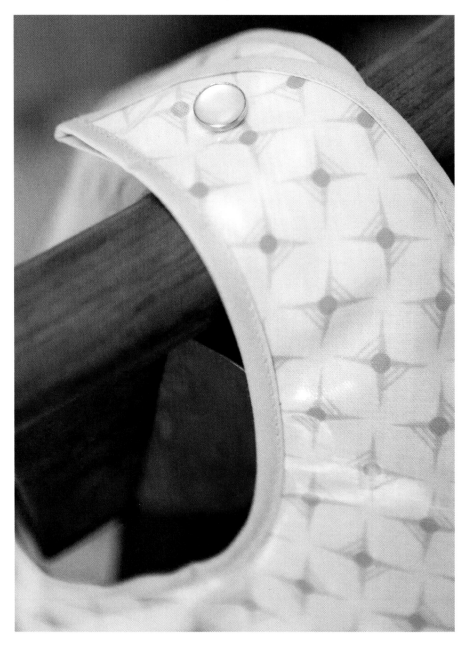

Splat Mat

Splat Mat

Finished Dimensions: 4' × 4'

Every momma needs a splat mat or two to protect her floors. This mat starts out on the floor to catch all the food that baby enjoys tossing around, and it can hang around through the toddler years to protect the floor under the easel. Give it a good wipe-down and place it up on the table for finger painting and play dough time. Combine this with a baby bib or an art smock and you've got the best shower or birthday gift ever!

> **June Suggests:** You know your space best, so make the mat as big or as little as you need.

Materials

Note: Oilcloth contains phthalates and is not to be used for projects intended for children under the age of 12 or for projects that come in direct contact with food, so this project uses laminated cotton. Please do not substitute oilcloth for this project.

1 1/2 yards 54"/56" laminated cotton for splat mat
Two packages of contrasting 1/2" double-fold bias tape
Matching thread
Rotary cutter (optional)
Cutting mat (optional)
Clear ruler

Mark It Up and Cut It Out

1. Prep your fabric by removing the selvedge from one side of your laminated cotton. Be sure to cut the edge in a straight line because this is one of the edges of your splat mat. This is a great job for a rotary cutter, cutting mat, and clear ruler.

2. Use your wide ruler to mark your first corner off the edge you just cut, making sure it's a 90° angle. From this mark extend the line 48" and then create another corner. Repeat the process until you've drawn a 4' square.

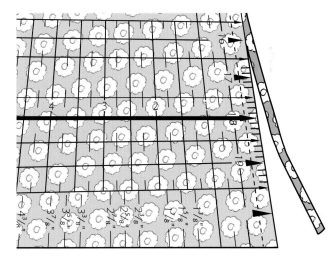

Steps

1. Connect the two packages of bias into one 6-yard strip of bias tape. (See pages 10–11 for information about working with bias tape.)

2. Start trimming your splat mat about 6" away from a corner by sandwiching your ½" bias tape around the edge of your mat. Pin and then edge stitch into place until you reach a corner.

3. At the corner, create a faux mitered corner (see page 12 for information on creating a faux mitered corner). Pin the next side and stitch. Repeat until the last corner.

4. After you have made your last corner, trim the end of the tape so that about 1½" overlaps beyond the starting point. Make a ½" fold in the end of the tape so that the raw end is tucked in. Sandwich the remainder of the bias in place, overlapping the starting point. Pin into place and sew.

5. Now lay that pretty mat out on the floor and let the kids be messy while you rejoice that your floors are protected.

Art Smock

Art Smock

Finished Measurements: Fits 3T-5T (11" at chest and 14¼" long)

This simple art smock made out of soft and waterproof laminated cotton is momma's best friend. Its full coverage keeps your artist clean and dry. Clean up is a breeze; just wipe with a damp sponge and hang to dry.

June Suggests: I know that boys like to do art, too; just straighten out the curves on the patterns to make one of these for a little guy.

Materials

Note: Oilcloth contains phthalates and is not to be used for projects intended for children under the age of 12 or for projects that come in direct contact with food, so this project uses laminated cotton. Please do not substitute oilcloth for this project.

½ yard of 44"/45" or 54"/56" laminated cotton for smock

¼ yard of 44"/45" or 54"/56" laminated cotton for pocket

2 packages of contrasting ½" double-fold bias tape for the pocket, outer smock edging, and side ties

1 package of contrasting ¼" double-fold bias tape for the neckline edging and ties

Coordinating thread

Note: The instructions call for contrasting prints but the laminated cotton used for the sample was so cute I used it for the pocket, too. Feel free to mix and match your prints or use a single print.

Mark It Up and Cut It Out

1. Photocopy the patterns on pages 140–142. Make sure to enlarge them by the percentage printed on the pattern pieces and cut the number of pieces indicated on the patterns.

2. Mark the notches for the pocket and ties onto the smock front and use a pencil to lightly draw the 6" center stitch line for the pocket on the back of the smock.

3. Mark the notch for the ties and draw the 3½" line at the neckline (which is the placket) on the smock back.

Steps

1. Cut 16" of ½" double-fold bias tape and sandwich the tape along the top edge of the pocket. Edge stitch it into place. (See the edge stitch tip on page 9.)

2. Pin the pocket along the bottom of the art smock front, matching up the top of the pocket with the notch you drew on the fabric. The wrong side of the pocket should be facing the right side of the smock front piece. Baste stitch the pocket in place, ⅛" from the edge. (See the illustration.)

Step 2

Back

Step 4

3. Working on the wrong side of the smock front, stitch along the center line to divide the pocket into two separate pockets. Pin the pocket in place by placing the pins right along the stitch line. Be sure to backstitch at the top of the pocket for added strength. (See the illustration.)

Wrong side of smock front

Step 3

4. Using scissors, cut a slit along the line that you drew onto the smock back. Now trim this placket with a 7½" piece of ¼" double-fold bias tape. Your slit is now a V-shaped opening. (See the illustration.)

5. With the right sides together, pin the front and the back of the smock together at the shoulders and stitch using a ½" seam allowance.

6. Finger press (see page 9 for a tip on finger pressing) the shoulder seams toward the back and understitch the seam in place (read about understitching on page 10).

7. Create your side ties by cutting four 18" strips of ½" double-fold bias tape. Sew the bias tape ties closed being sure that one end of each tie is finished off. Refer to page 11 for details on finishing off cotton bias tape.

8. Pin the unfinished end of each of the ties to each side of the smock front and back at the notches you marked. The ties should lie over the smock pieces toward the center. (See the illustration.) Stitch the ties in place.

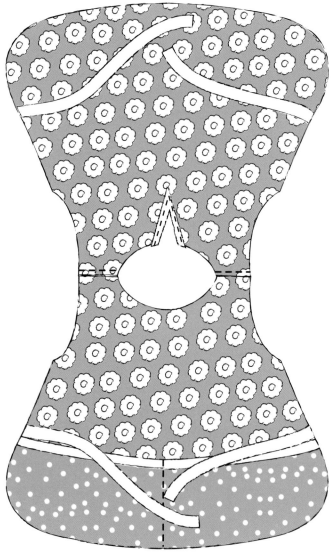

Step 8

9. Cut a 52" piece of ¼" double-fold bias tape. Sandwich the bias tape along the neckline and edge stitch it in place, leaving 18" ties at each end to create the ties for the neckline of the smock. (See the illustration.) Fold the ends of the bias inside its own folds for a finished end to each tie.

11. Fold the ties over the trim and stitch along the same stitch line you used to stitch the trim. (See the illustration.)

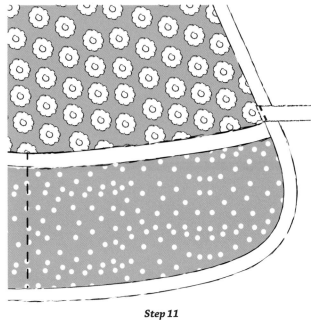

Step 11

12. Now your little artist can get to work on the next masterpiece.

Step 9

10. Trim the entire art smock with a 96" piece of the ½" double-fold bias tape, turning the last bit under to finish it off nicely. (Refer to page 11 for information about finishing trim.)

Mommy
and Me
Aprons

Mommy and Me Aprons

Finished Measurements: Child's apron fits 3T-5T. Woman's apron fits sizes 4-14.

What mommy doesn't want to create memories of cooking with her little sweeties? This Mommy and Me apron set is sure to help. These full-coverage bib aprons are wider at the hips to help keep both of you clean. The integrated pockets are flattering for mom and let the kiddos hold lots of loot. I love that it takes very little laminated cotton to make a set of waterproof aprons. Wouldn't these make a thoughtful and economical gift?

> June Suggests: Grab two yards of laminated cotton and mix and match the prints. That way Mommy's apron matches Tot's pockets and Tot's apron matches Mommy's pockets. Or go simple, and one yard of laminated cotton is all you need to make both aprons if you don't want to use a contrasting print.

Materials

Note: Oilcloth contains phthalates and is not to be used for projects intended for children under the age of 12 or for projects that come in direct contact with food, so this project uses laminated cotton. Please do not substitute oilcloth for this project.

1 yard of 54"/56" laminated cotton for the aprons (Patterns A and C)

$^3/_8$ yard of 54"/56" laminated cotton for the pocket (Patterns B and D) and the U-shaped neck/shoulder strap (Patterns E and F)

3 packages (all the same color) of contrasting $^1/_2$" double-fold bias tape for the side binding and ties

2 packages (both the same color) of contrasting $^1/_4$" double-fold bias tape for the top, pocket, and bottom binding

2 packages of $^1/_4$" rickrack

Coordinating threads

Mark It Up and Cut It Out

1. Photocopy pattern pieces A, B, C, D, E, and F from pages 143–150 making sure to increase them by the percentage noted on each piece. Cut out the pattern pieces.

2. Fold the selvedge ends of your 1-yard piece of laminated cotton in so the wrong sides are facing out, align patterns A and C at the fold then trace and cut.

3. Fold your ⅜-yard piece of laminated cotton in half. Trace the pocket pieces (B and D) and U-shaped neck/shoulder straps (E and F) on the fabric and cut through both layers.

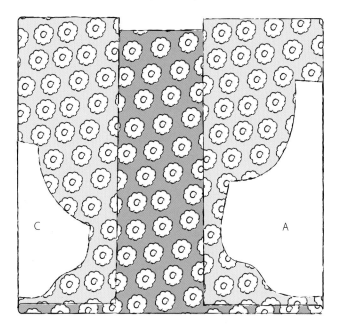

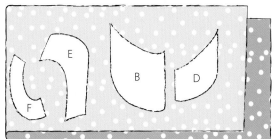

4. Mark the notches for the trim, pocket, and strap placement on both the apron pieces.

Steps

1. Starting at the notch and working toward the corner, sandwich your ¼" bias tape along the sides of the aprons where the pockets will be. Edge stitch (see the edge stitch tip on page 9) from the side of the apron to the notch. (See the illustration.)

Note: If you want to cut your bias tape before applying it, cut 11" for a tot apron and 14" for a mommy apron.

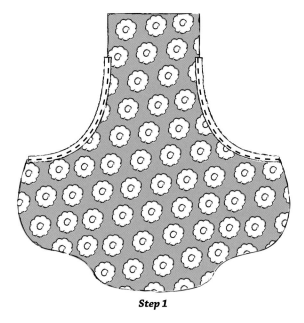

Step 1

2. Pin the rickrack to the edge of the bias, right along the stitch line. Use the matching thread to sew right through the center of the rickrack.

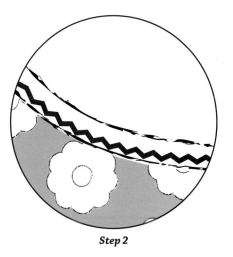

Step 2

4. Turn the aprons right side up and pin the ¼" bias tape along the edges of the top of the aprons' bibs and also along the hems of the aprons. Edge stitch it in place. (See the illustration.)

5. Layer the mini rickrack on top of the ½" bias tape to finish the bottom and top edges of the aprons. Pin and then edge stitch into place as you did in Step 2.

3. Turn your aprons right side down and place the pockets right side down on top of the aprons. Match the bottoms of the pockets to the notches on the sides of the aprons and the tops of the pockets with the tops of the ¼" trim that you applied in Step 1. (Remember, pinning into laminated cotton can leave holes, so be sure to pin only along the stitch lines on the back of the pockets and at the side of the pockets. See page 10 for tips on using glue sticks instead of pins with laminated cotton.) Stitch the pockets in place, ½" from the curved pocket edges as shown in the illustration.

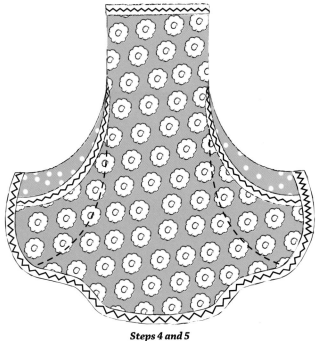

Steps 4 and 5

6. To create the neck/shoulder strap, pin the two Pattern E pieces together with the right sides facing (see the illustration). Do the same with the two Pattern F pieces. Stitch the pieces together to form a U and iron the seam open. (See how to iron with laminated cotton on page 9.)

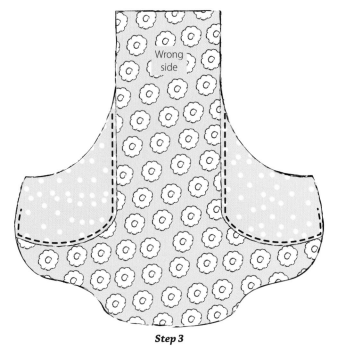

Wrong side

Step 3

7. Apply ½" bias and rickrack along the inside curve of the neck and shoulder piece.

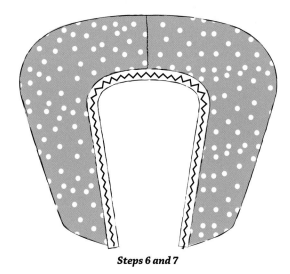

Steps 6 and 7

8. Lay the U-shaped neck/shoulder piece onto a work space face up and then lay the bib of the apron right side up on the shoulder piece. The top of the apron bib should overlap the straps by ½". Pin and sew along the same stitch line that you stitched to attach the rickrack to the bib of the aprons.

9. Create ties for the mommy apron by cutting one 114" piece of ½" bias tape, which gives you 26" ties at the neck and the waist and also covers the unfinished edge of the bib and the top of the pocket. See page 10 for instructions on extending cotton bias tape if your bias isn't long enough.

10. Take the 114" piece of bias and measure 26" from one end, marking the point with a straight pin. Measure 26" from the other end and mark it with a straight pin.

11. Sandwich the middle section of the trim along the sides of the bib and around the outside curve of the neck and shoulder piece and then back down the other side. Pin the trim in place, and then sew the entire length of bias shut from end to end. An edge stitch works well in this situation. Be sure to backstitch at the stress point of the ties (where the ties meet up with the apron). See the illustration.

12. Trim the bias you just applied with the ¼" rickrack. Start at the corner of one pocket, turn ¼" under and pin in place, continue up the bib of the apron and around the neck and shoulder piece, and then go down the other side of the apron. Stop at the end of the second pocket where the ties begin. Sew the rickrack in place. (See the illustration.)

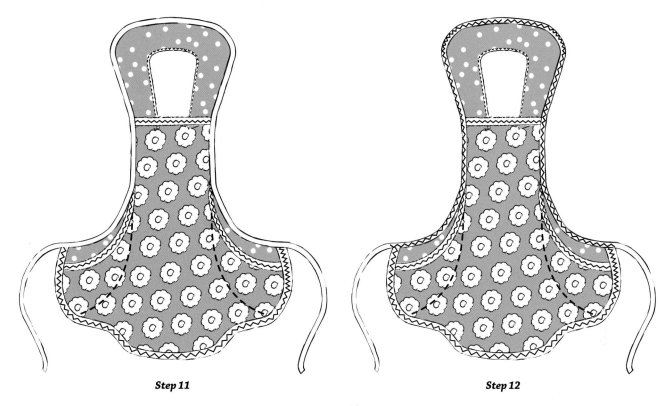

Step 11   *Step 12*

13. Repeat Steps 5 through 7 for the tot apron using one 80" piece of ½" bias tape and measuring 19" from each end of the bias.

14. Now it's time for you and your little cook to make some cookies and some very special memories.

Pattern Pieces

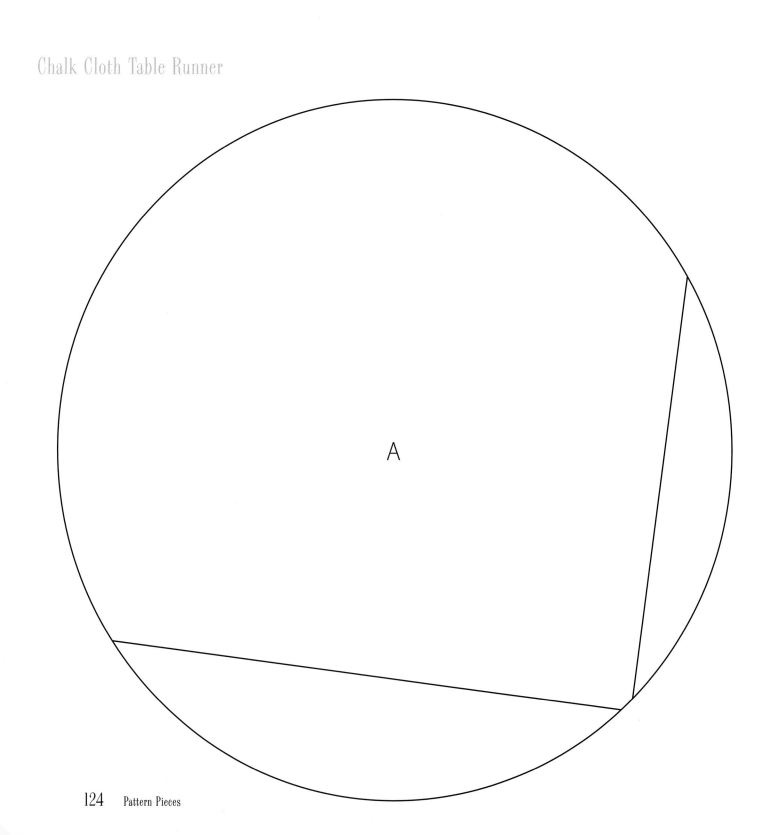

A

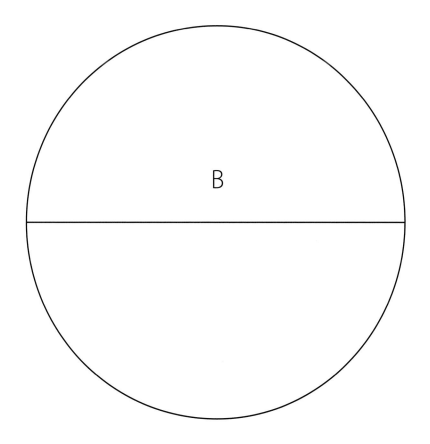

B

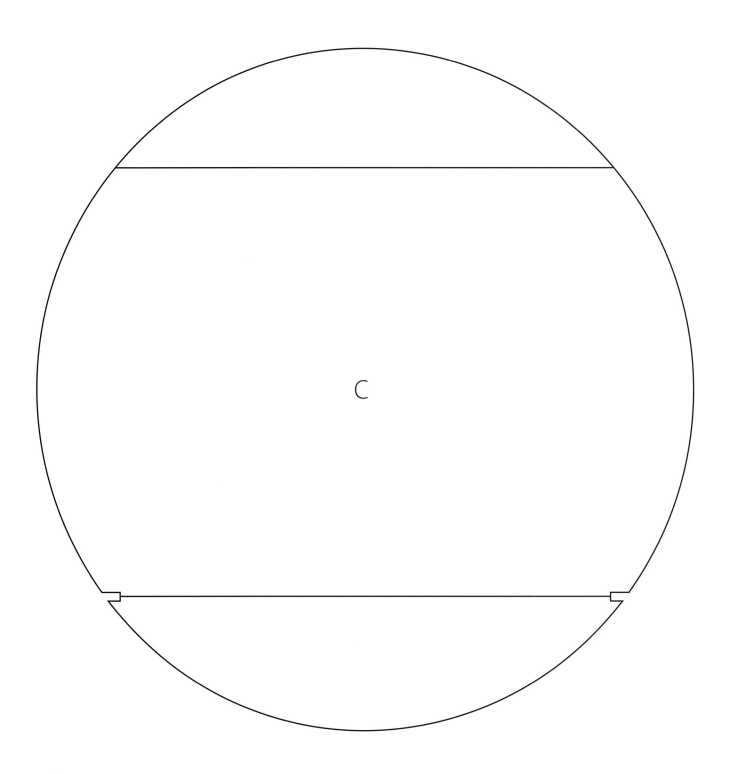

C

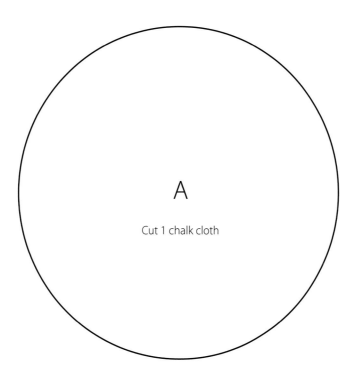

A

Cut 1 chalk cloth

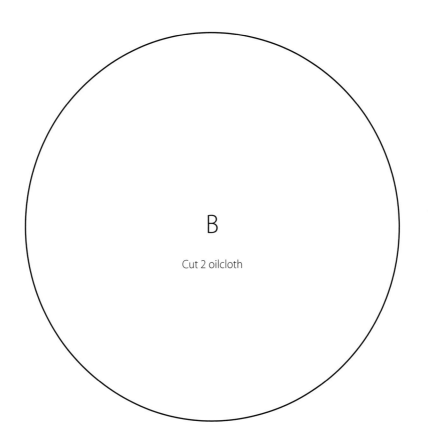

B

Cut 2 oilcloth

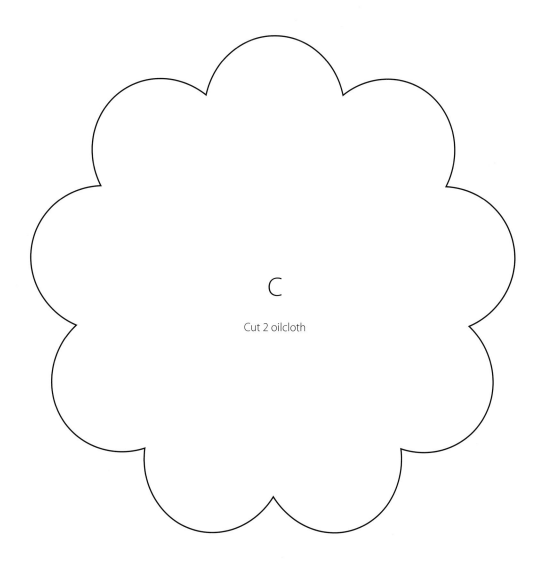

C

Cut 2 oilcloth

Pillow Cover

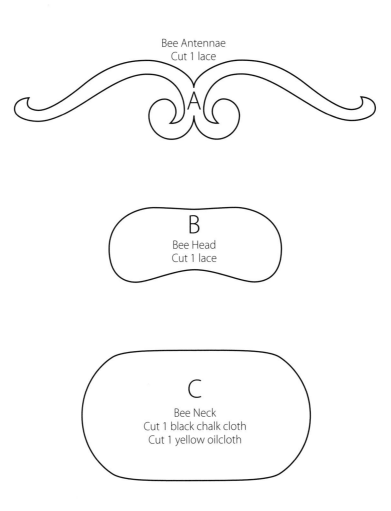

Bee Antennae
Cut 1 lace

A

B
Bee Head
Cut 1 lace

C

Bee Neck
Cut 1 black chalk cloth
Cut 1 yellow oilcloth

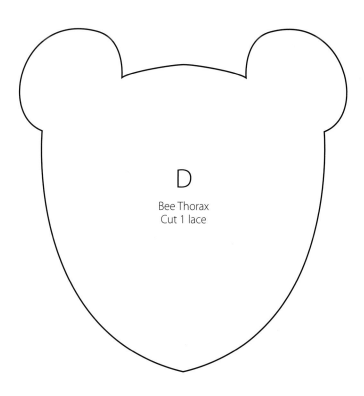

D

Bee Thorax
Cut 1 lace

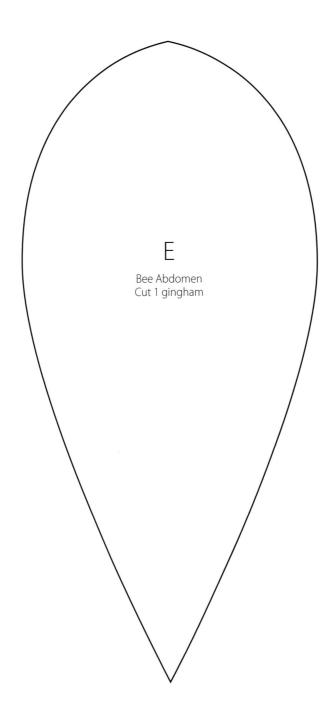

E

Bee Abdomen
Cut 1 gingham

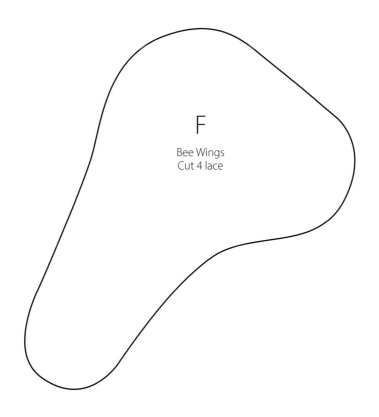

F

Bee Wings
Cut 4 lace

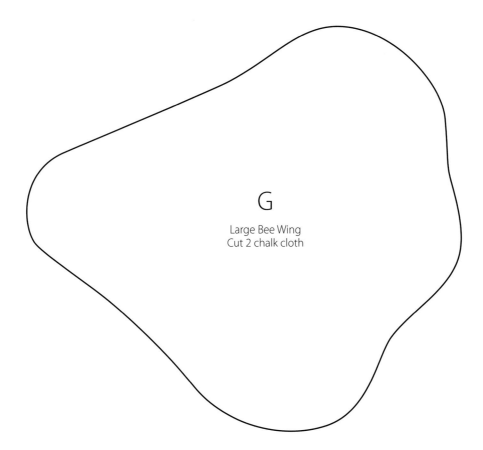

G

Large Bee Wing
Cut 2 chalk cloth

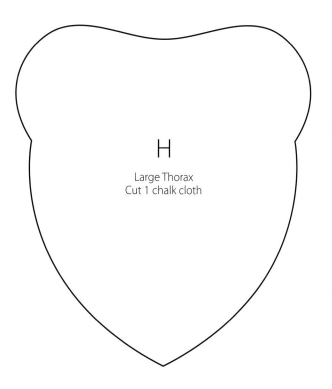

H

Large Thorax
Cut 1 chalk cloth

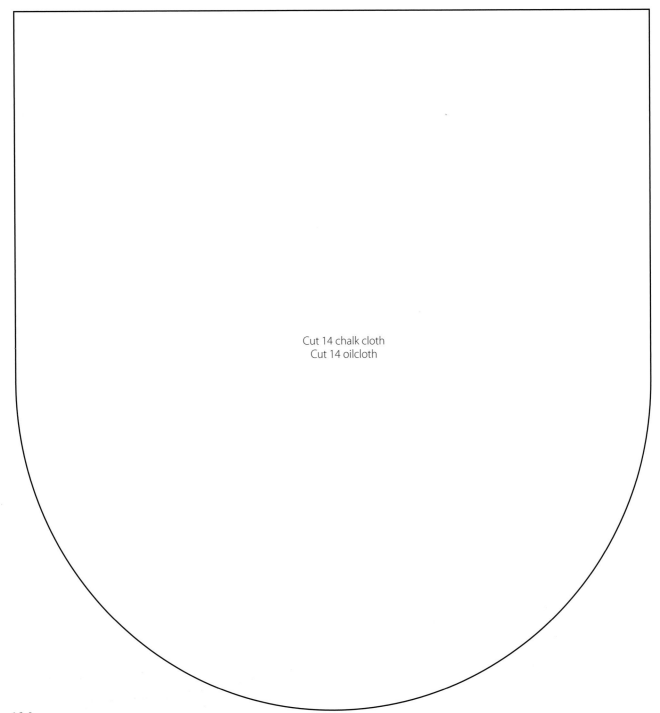

Cut 14 chalk cloth
Cut 14 oilcloth

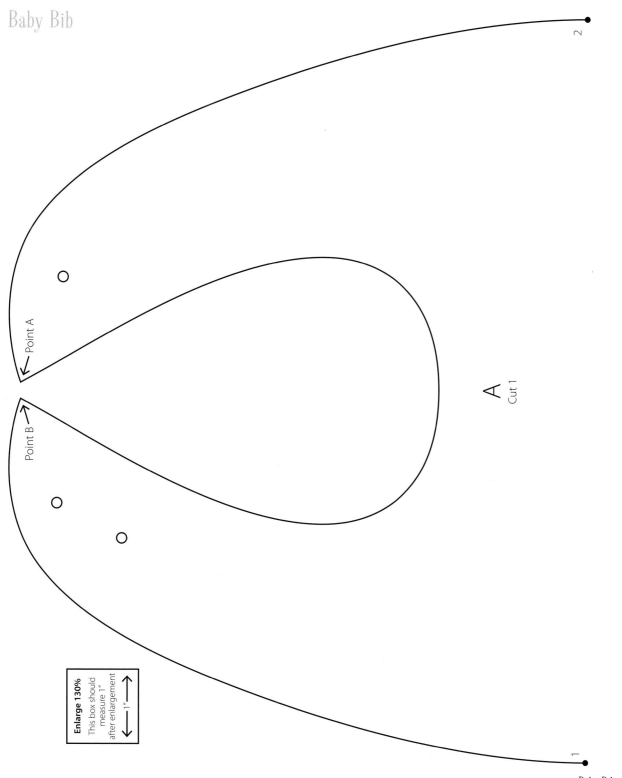

Point A

Point B

A
Cut 1

2

1

Enlarge 130%
This box should
measure 1"
after enlargement

1"

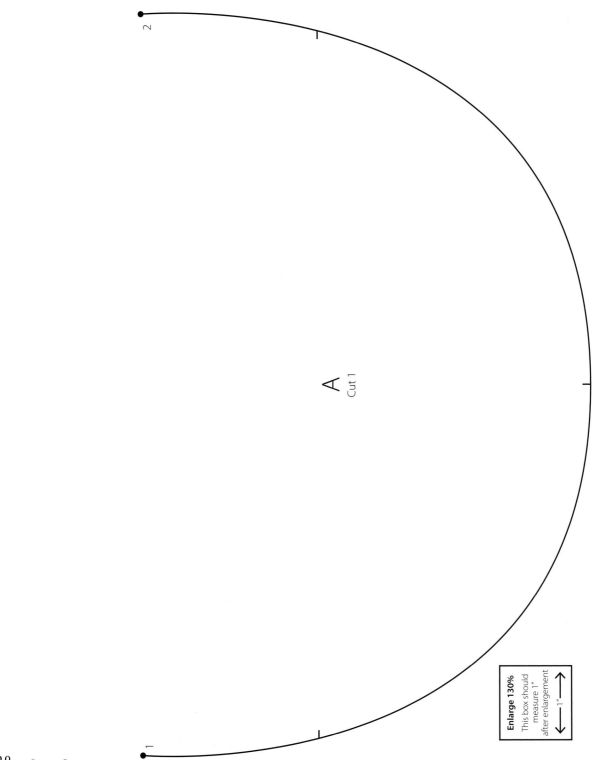

2

1

A
Cut 1

Enlarge 130%
This box should
measure 1"
after enlargement

1"

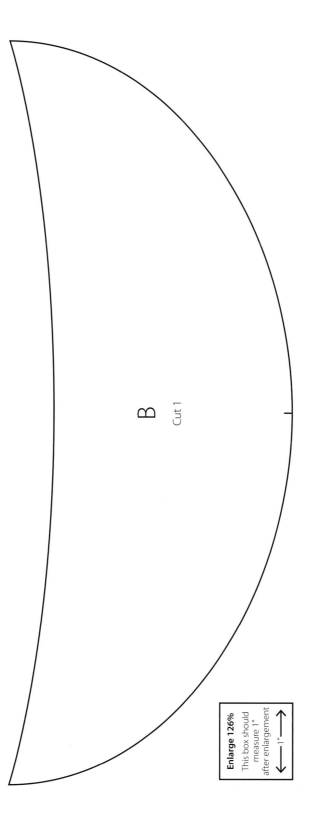

B

Cut 1

Enlarge 126%
This box should
measure 1"
after enlargement

↕ 1"

Art Smock

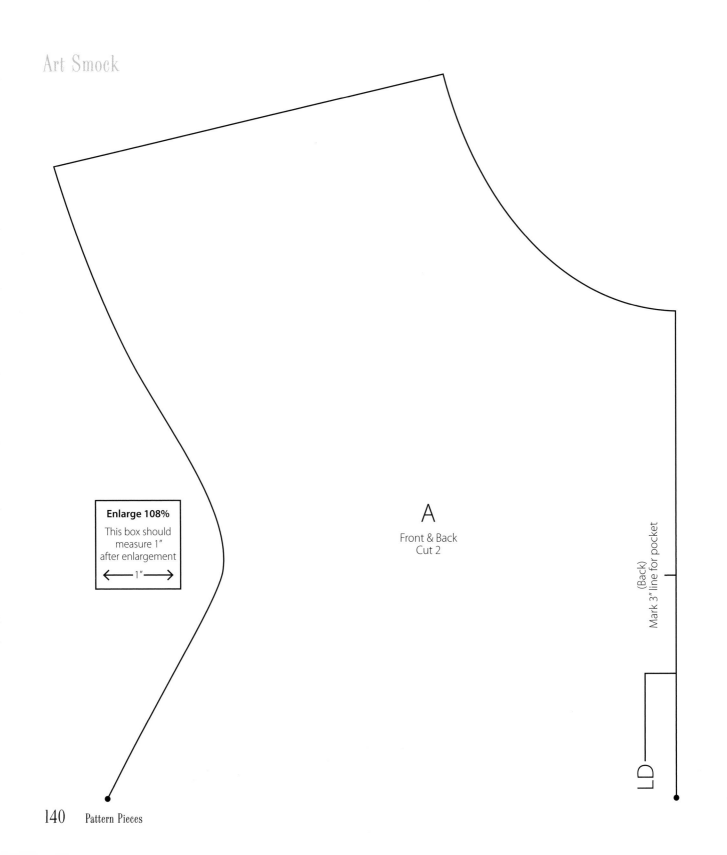

Enlarge 108%

This box should
measure 1"
after enlargement

← 1" →

A

Front & Back
Cut 2

(Back)
Mark 3" line for pocket

LD

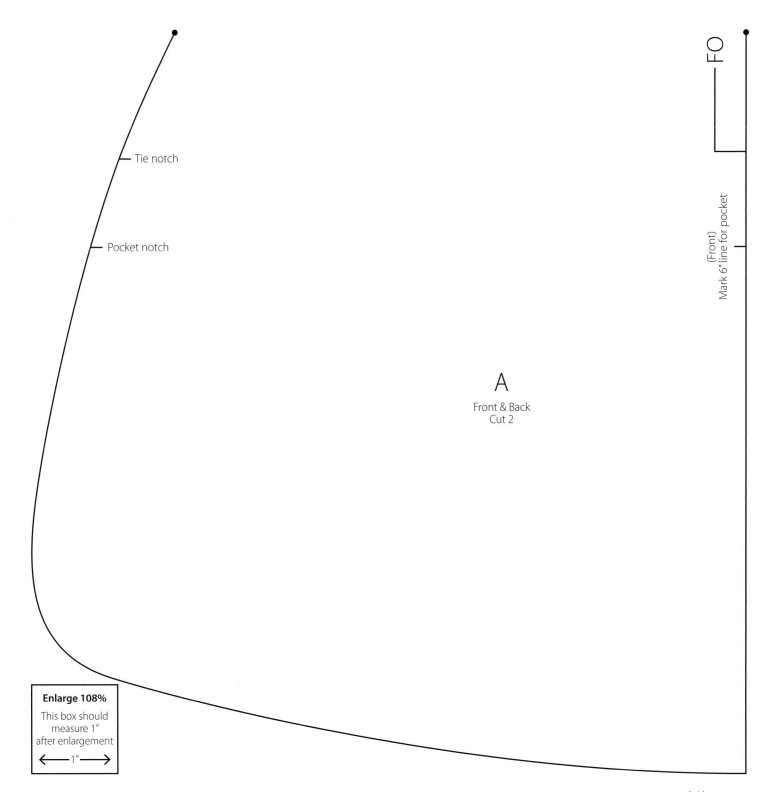

Tie notch

Pocket notch

A
Front & Back
Cut 2

FO

(Front)
Mark 6" line for pocket

Enlarge 108%

This box should
measure 1"
after enlargement

⟵ 1" ⟶

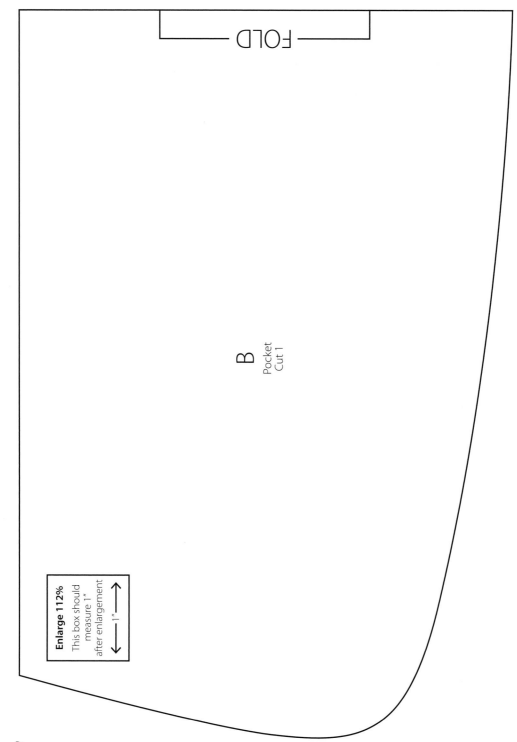

FOLD

B

Pocket
Cut 1

Enlarge 112%

This box should
measure 1"
after enlargement

1"

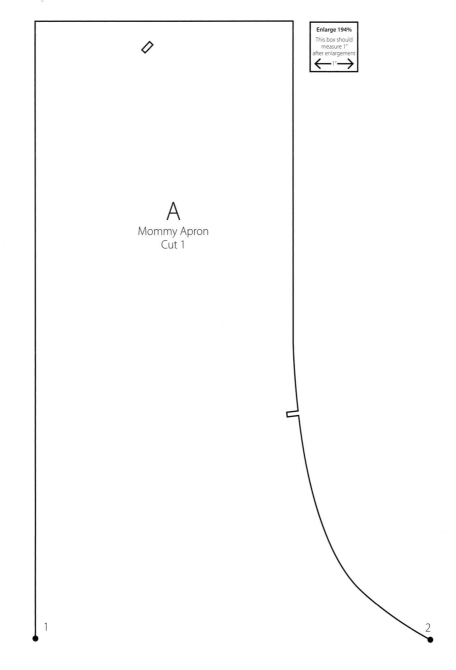

A
Mommy Apron
Cut 1

Enlarge 194%
This box should
measure 1"
after enlargement
← 1" →

1

2

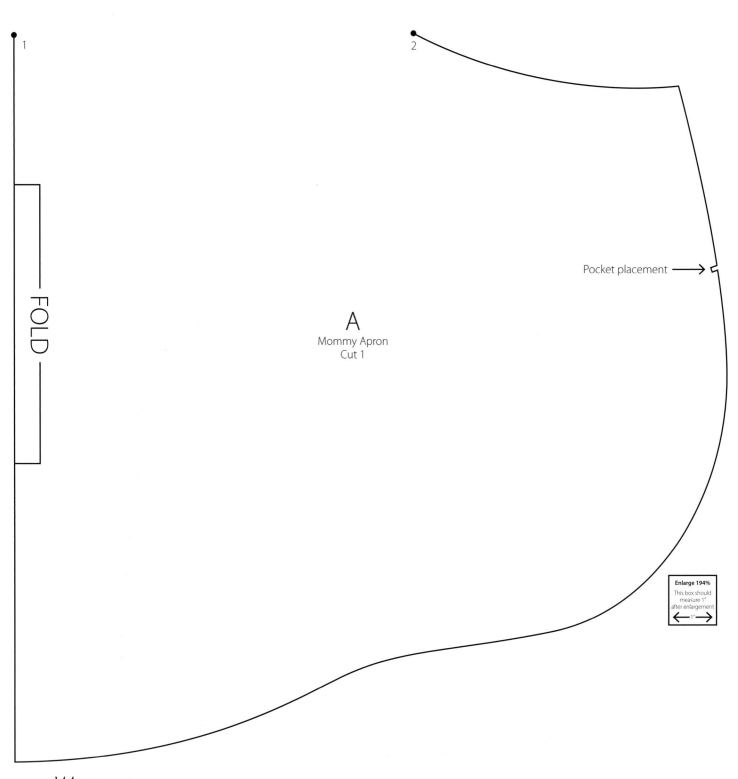

1

2

FOLD

A
Mommy Apron
Cut 1

Pocket placement

Enlarge 194%
This box should
measure 1"
after enlargement
←— 1" —→

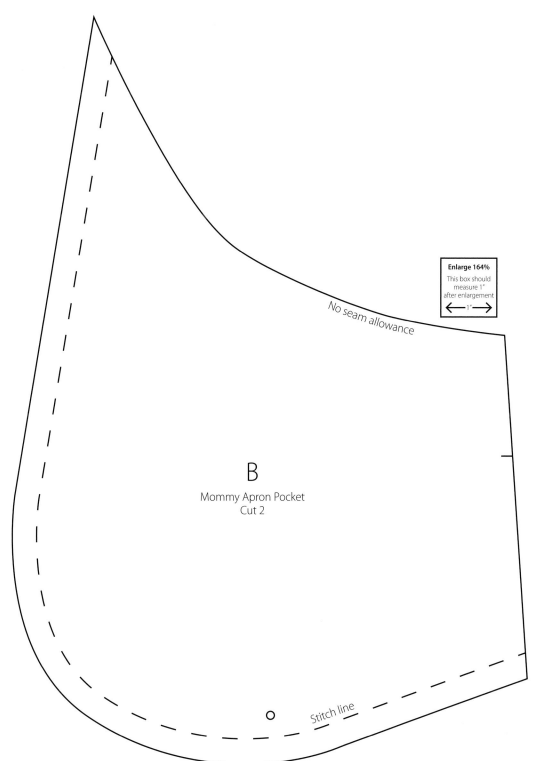

B

Mommy Apron Pocket
Cut 2

No seam allowance

Stitch line

Enlarge 164%

This box should
measure 1"
after enlargement

← 1" →

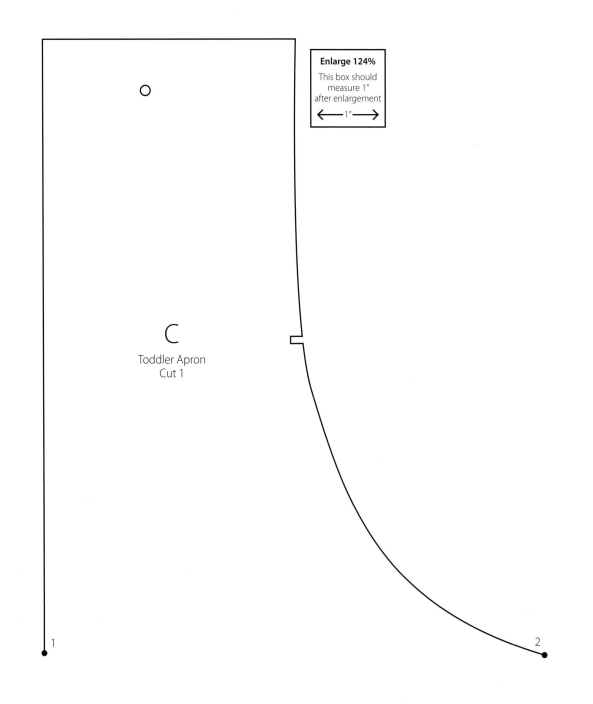

Enlarge 124%

This box should measure 1″ after enlargement

←——— 1″ ———→

C

Toddler Apron
Cut 1

1

2

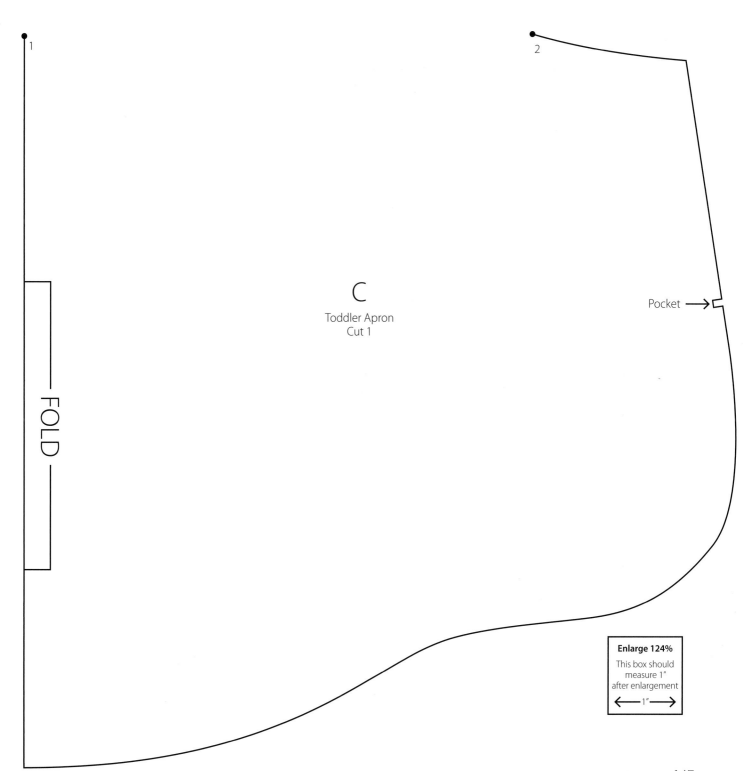

1

2

FOLD

C

Toddler Apron
Cut 1

Pocket →

Enlarge 124%

This box should
measure 1″
after enlargement

←— 1″ —→

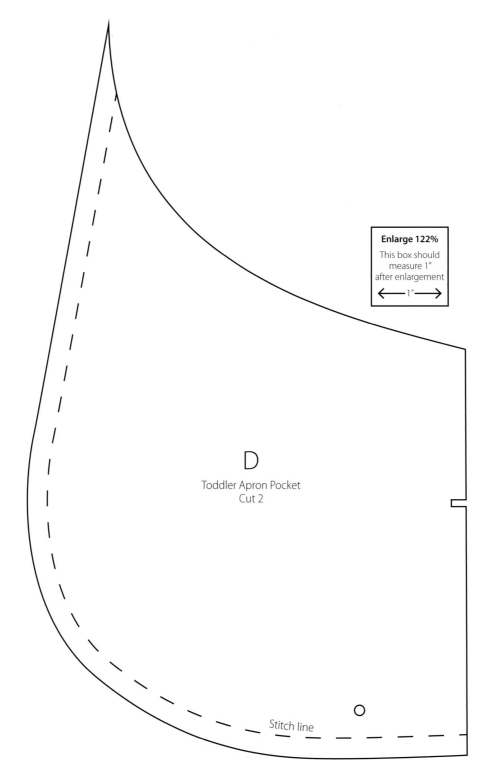

Enlarge 122%

This box should
measure 1"
after enlargement

⟵—1"—⟶

D

Toddler Apron Pocket
Cut 2

Stitch line

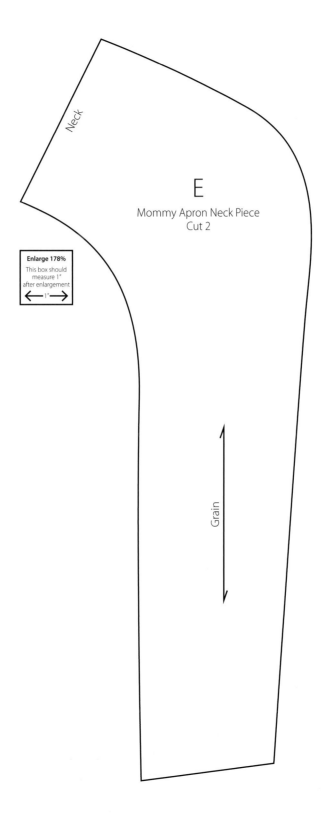

Neck

E

Mommy Apron Neck Piece
Cut 2

Enlarge 178%
This box should
measure 1"
after enlargement

←— 1" —→

Grain

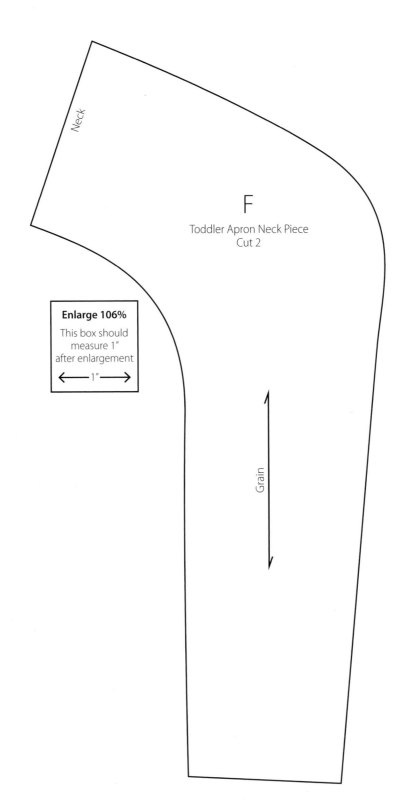

Neck

F

Toddler Apron Neck Piece
Cut 2

Enlarge 106%

This box should
measure 1"
after enlargement

←——— 1" ———→

Grain

Index